CATAPULT

CATAPULT

A WOMAN'S GUIDE TO BUILDING A 7-FIGURE BUSINESS

ABBIE WIDIN, PHD

First published 2014

Typeset in Mercury 11pt Text G1 Roman
Copyright © Abbie Widin

The moral rights of the Author have been asserted

National Library of Australia Cataloguing-in-Publication entry
Author: Widin, Abbie.
Title: Catapult: A woman's guide to building a 7-figure business / Abbie Widin
ISBN: 978-0-9924882-0-8 (pbk)
Subjects: Entrepreneurship; Women and Business; Success in Business – Psychological aspects

Cover design by Vanessa Maynard
Edited by Nikki Griffin

Disclaimer

This book is available at special quantity discounts to use as premiums and sales promotions, or for use in training programs. To contact us, please email us at info@oneextrazero.com

To Melinda, Amelie, Thalia and Lachlan

TABLE OF CONTENTS

ABOUT THE AUTHOR

Abbie Widin, Ph.D., is the principal of One Extra Zero and specializes in helping ambitious women service providers significantly grow their business and themselves.

Through her keynote speeches, workshops, mentoring, writing and coaching, she transforms the lives of women business owners.

Abbie believes that being successful in business allows women to become the person they always wanted to be, but weren't quite sure that they could become.

Abbie has a marketing and management background in building 9-figure businesses with 8-figure marketing budgets with companies such as Procter & Gamble and Kellogg, and brings an energetic intensity to everything she does.

INTRODUCTION

I wrote this book because I needed to accelerate my own understanding about the mindsets of women who had created successful businesses from scratch.

Before I started my own business, I had been managing nine-figure businesses and spending eight-figure budgets. I had a certain mindset and capacity that allowed me to thrive in that environment. But to be clear, I was managing an existing business. There were established stakeholders and customers and layers of management above me, and the trailblazers who created the business were long gone.

BEING A 7-FIGURE BUSINESS OWNER IS DIFFERENT

My long-supressed feminism started to rise up. I found myself discovering more about the gender and financial gaps in entrepreneurial success, combined with a mega-trend of women starting their own businesses. I realised that I wanted to take the business planning disciplines and the sales and marketing skills that I'd developed in big American multi-nationals and help more women make more money.

I quickly found that whilst many skills are transferable, there were others that I needed to pick up, and pick up quickly.

I WORK WITH MANY WOMEN IN BUSINESS

Women are starting their own businesses at a faster rate than ever before, even at a faster rate than men. They want to be their own boss, to have work/life balance and flexibility. However, on average for all women business owners, fewer than half draw an income from their business, and only about one-third of women sole-traders do.

In the US, only 12% of female-owned businesses turnover more than $100,000 per year, and only 1.8% turnover more than $1,000,000 per year. As a total business aggregate only 0.5% female-owned businesses turnover more than $1,000,000 out of all businesses.

WOMEN DON'T ALWAYS LEAN IN

Whilst women are starting businesses at a faster rate than men, we still don't do quite as well as we should. We don't always lean in at the table of entrepreneurs.

We struggle with issues of self-worth. Quite often, we wait for business to come to us instead of going out there and getting it for ourselves. We don't like talking about our fees. We aren't always charging enough for our services. We want to give so much that we end up over-delivering. We run the risk of burnout when we work long hours for too little money. We don't always bounce back from a challenge or obstacle. Sometimes we think the first no is the final one.

MOVING FROM TECHNICIAN TO CEO

Women often start businesses *in* areas that they have experience in, and end up working more in their business than *on* their business. Becoming a leader is critical to success, taking control of the direction of the business, being able to communicate our vision and enrolling others to help us get there. We don't always recognise our own strengths and so we don't implement systems that would allow us to step away from pure operations and take on a leadership role.

THE PRINCIPLES THAT GET YOU FROM START-UP TO SIX-FIGURES AND THEN SEVEN-FIGURES

The women who come to me are looking for growth in their businesses. Whether they are almost at 6-figures, have passed 6-figures or are well on their way to seven-figures, they are stuck.

That's because challenges that we face when a business is in start-up are different to those faced by an established or larger business. For a start-up, challenges are often focused around defining your niche and managing cash flow whilst actively looking for each new customer. It is a journey of faith, and very often you have to believe that the results will come before you see them.

The mindset and practical skill sets that propel you through each level of revenue in your business must continue to evolve as you level up. Your current mindset and belief in your own possibility is based on your previous experiences. To reach the next level, you need to create a new mindset; one that allows the possibility of further growth to be believed.

Once a woman has successfully brought her business turn-over to the range of $100,000-$250,000, she finds different challenges. At this level she'll find that her biggest challenges are in the way that she manages time and systems. She will be busy, usually without enough support, and she'll find that things start to fall through the cracks.

At around the $350,000-$500,000 mark, she'll need additional systems and processes in place to allow her to leverage her time. She might have a team around her, and a clear plan for where future business will come from. However, she will still need to bust through her beliefs around her ability to grow beyond that level.

Once she breaks through the seven-figure mark, the challenges (unfortunately) don't vanish. The practical business-building challenges focus even more on her time and the numbers, where small adjustments can have a big impact. And again, the mindset that allows her to continue to seek growth must continue to evolve.

During my own journey, I realised that there was a gap in the market, and a real need for business income acceleration help that focused on both the mindset and practical business building advice for women.

Having an impeccable resume is no guarantee of success. The factors that help women excel in the corporate environment have a good overlap with those required for entrepreneurship, but they are nowhere close to identical.

For me, the biggest challenge was moving from selling something else to selling myself. Even if you are moderately capable of promoting yourself internally to get recognition and promotions, promoting yourself to an external audience is different, and requires a different skillset and mindset.

I found that I needed to put my own abilities and results out there for the world to see, and then stand up and say, "I'm capable of doing all that and better."

The other thing that I learned quickly was that whilst having entrepreneurial parents was good modelling, there was no guarantee that their experiences and expertise would be passed on.

The rewards that you enjoy as a child do not simply continue to flow as you age. You need to do the work yourself. As you do the work, you'll gain a new respect for yourself.

MY PURPOSE

My purpose in life is to live with intention and integrity. To nurture myself and my family, and to empower other women to fly with their own wings.

I am intentional and deliberate about how I spend my time. I only have so much! Living with integrity is just part of my DNA, and means that I am not only honest and trustworthy, but my decisions and actions are aligned internally with what I believe and what I do.

Creating independence is so very important to me. It's the final stage in a woman's evolution. In which she learns to fly with her own wings and live a life of desire, purpose and independence rather than compromise.

The women who were interviewed in this book represent a broad cross-section of demographics that had built successful businesses in the service industry such as social media, graphic design and branding, as well as massage and medical spa services. Other service businesses include management consulting, recruitment and coaching.

It became very clear to me that it was not the demographics that were important in creating a million dollar business. There were no variables in common.

Some women had in their first million dollar turnover year whilst still in their twenties, others 'arrived' in their late forties. Some came from working class families, while others came from more well-heeled stock. Some women were single, some married. Some had children, some without.

Despite these demographic differences, the key principles that drove their success were very clear:

1. They were connected to their purpose and their purpose was aligned with their business. Each woman knew why she was doing what she was doing.

2. Total responsibility. Not only did these women know that they couldn't give up, but they took responsibility for their business model, the size and the structure of the business.

3. They had a vision of what their business could become, and stretched themselves to triple that vision. They also figured out whom they needed to broadly share the vision with.

4. They recognised that they would be personally challenged, and surrounded themselves in an

environment that supported their transformation and growth.

5. They recognised that fear and doubt had to be overcome, and developed strategies and resources to continue moving through and past fear. This enabled them to be visible where they might not otherwise.

6. Money was an energetic reward for their efforts. And to become more skilled at attracting money, they practiced not only their mindset, but also developing their practical skills.

7. Time and team were the keys to their leverage. As your business grows, you can't do everything yourself, you simply cannot continue to grow your impact without breaking!

This book is laid out to expand upon each of these key success principles. The first half of each chapter is designed to help you nurture a specific mindset. The latter half is called "Down to Business" and gives practical business building steps for each principle.

At the end of each chapter is a summary of the essential points of the chapter, as well as a link to download bonuses. These bonuses provide a way to assess where you are and to give ways of exploring and guiding your beliefs around each area.

I created this book because I believe that women need to learn what it takes to build a business that turns more than $1 million dollars a year. Finding your financial independence is your own journey. But, for many women, having your own business is one of the surest ways of getting there.

I believe that you're worthy of it!

CHAPTER 1

LIVE YOUR LIFE AND BUSINESS ON PURPOSE

"Our lives become very powerful when we are operating from a sense of true purpose. On purpose we naturally work on task, we naturally want to acquire more knowledge, we naturally want to excel and be the best we can be. But it all takes a solid foundation of purpose, without it we are just patching up old problems temporarily and hoping for the best!"
— Tina Olivero

START WITH YOUR WHY

Growing a successful business is hugely rewarding, but to get there, it is inevitable that you will face struggles and challenges along the way. However, when you know that your business is designed around your purpose, and that what you do is important to the world, then you are connecting with a higher purpose, a force bigger than yourself. That connection allows you to continue on in the face of challenges, and to overcome fear and doubt. It will even give you the strength to get back up again when you're knocked down. It is the "Why" you do what you do.

Kendall Summer Hawk has built a $3 million coaching and mentoring business with a focus on money, marketing, and soul.

My business is in total alignment with my life purpose: "to love and be loved." When it comes to my business purpose, "it is for women to love who and what they are and what they're doing and to make fabulous money doing it." When I'm out of alignment, I'm doubting myself and talking myself out of listening to my intuition, talking myself down, struggling, and wasting huge amounts of time and energy.

When women feel that integrated with who they are and what they're doing, they become unstoppable. And not just outwardly, but unstoppable inwardly in their connection to their brilliance, their magnificence, and their sense of purpose on the planet. They just walk in grace, and they are in grace. My vision is for every woman to walk in her own persona of being in this place of grace with herself.

It is important to know why you are have chosen this particular path in your life. Being mindful of your choices gives you a chance to be deliberate and intentional with your time. It's very easy to simply go with the flow, to hang up your shingle in an area that you know well, or in which you've developed some practical skills. But it is much more rewarding to combine that with something that brings you joy and follow that path instead. It is a challenge to step out of your comfort zone, but the rewards will outweigh the difficulties.

Being connected with your greater purpose will allow you to carry on when things get rough, because you know that you have an anchor point in the universe. When the cross-current tides start to get stronger, and the waves are buffeting you about, you will have your greater purpose to guide you. Like a lighthouse, your purpose becomes a beacon leading you through the dark.

Sophie Bartho built a $1.5 million creative design and branding agency from scratch almost straight out of university.

"You have to know why you're doing it. You will constantly be challenged, and I think if you genuinely know why you're doing it, it'll keep you grounded and keep you going."

An excellent way of knowing whether you are living your purpose is to ask yourself: Do I look forward more to my working days or my days off? If you work in an environment where you find yourself counting down the hours until home time, then that is a good indication that you're not in a place where you are engaging in the big picture or following your greater purpose. Days off provide a necessary way to recharge and focus on other important areas of your life. But the ideal state is when you look forward to starting work as much, if not more than, your days off.

THE REASON WE NEED PURPOSE

There's a story of three bricklayers from the middle ages. They were toiling in the hot sun, all three of them brown and dusty, with the walls of the medieval town seen in the background. They were each asked what they were doing. The first answered, "I'm laying bricks, putting them in a line, and keeping them firm with mortar." The second answered, "I'm helping to build a building; it's good work that feeds my family." The third took a look around him, "I'm building a cathedral to celebrate the glory of god. This cathedral will stand for hundreds of years, and people will come from all corners to be part of the glory."

Internal motivation comes when you can see the greater meaning in even the most mundane tasks.

A TASK BY ITSELF IS HARD TO MAINTAIN

Let's say that you've decided to write a newsletter for your business. You know that other businesses do it, and decide that you should too. You'll most likely find that it's difficult to find the motivation to do a task just because you feel you should, and it's unlikely that you'll write more than two or three issues before giving up, because you've got no motivation or reason to continue.

A TASK IS EASIER IF LINKED TO A STRATEGY

If however, you are able to take a step back and look at the bigger picture, you will see that the task is part of a larger

strategy for your business. Your newsletter will nurture relationships with clients and keep the lines of communication
open. With that strategy in mind, it becomes easier to find
motivation to complete the task. You'll probably find that
you're able to get five or six newsletters out before your
motivation begins to wane. A strategy is stronger than a task
for providing motivation.

THE STRATEGY HAS LONGEVITY WHEN LINKED TO A GOAL

When your strategy is linked to a business goal, then the
tasks associated with that strategy start to have some lon-
gevity. When you have a greater sense of the bigger picture,
it becomes easier to follow through on tasks. You know that
if you write the newsletter, you'll stay in contact with your
prospective clients, and you'll be more likely to hit your
business goals. In this case, you might be able to keep your
newsletter going for a year or two.

YOU'LL BE UNSTOPPABLE WHEN THE GOAL IS LINKED TO YOUR PURPOSE

When your business goal is linked to your greater purpose,
you become unstoppable. If your business is designed to help
you make a contribution to the world, the task of writing the
newsletter becomes tied to your ability to get your message
out into the world. You'll feel compelled to get your message
out, to connect with the right people, and to reach them at a
time when they are most receptive.

Writing a newsletter is a task. Nurturing customers through on-going communication is a strategy. Building a business to a certain size is a goal. Fulfilling your greater purpose, and contributing to the world in a positive way is your Cathedral.

Shelene Taylor has built a string of massage centers and high-end medical spas with a combined turnover approaching $5 million. Shelene recommends finding your passion as a way of finding your purpose.

Get in touch and align with your passion, because what you have a passion for is your purpose. And being in touch with that will allow you to step forward and take the right action and keep putting one foot in front of the other, and never giving up on your dream. Always follow your dream and don't listen to other people who might say 'oh what about this' or 'what about that' or 'that's not a good idea'. Do it regardless. We know what's right for ourselves and when we're in alignment and following that passion, our purpose unfolds. Things show up for us that are truly magnificent and miraculous. Life is amazing and to live it to its fullest is what we're here to do.

WHAT WOULD YOU REGRET?

I often ask my clients a question: "In five years, in a professional sense, what would you regret not doing?" The answer is very often focused on wanting to expand their business or step into their potential. Overwhelmingly they want to have more of an impact in the world, and have the chance to do more good for other people.

What I rarely hear is: I just want to play it safe and make sure that I finish up with just enough.

Admittedly, I do work with women who are looking to grow their businesses and accelerate their income.

If people get stuck on their own answer to this question, it's usually because they don't have a clear sense of where they want to go. If that's the case for you, you can often find great clarity by considering your recent past. What do you regret not having done in the last five years?

CREATIVE SELF-EXPRESSION

When your business feels like a true expression of yourself, it allows you to bring to life the things that most make your heart sing.

Your business, vocation, or career is a crucial aspect of your life. It's a source of income and of contribution, and it should incorporate your talents and skills. More than that though, it should be an expression of your creativity and a source of joy.

Successful personal development blogger and author Steve Pavlina has a useful four-part model for understanding the role of creative self-expression in a business. He advocates a concept called "living congruently."

When the four areas of body, mind, heart and spirit are aligned, internal motivation occurs automatically because work no longer feels like a chore. As a natural consequence of finding this balance, you'll discover financial abundance, develop superior talent and find long-term fulfilment and a way to contribute meaningfully.

BODY – WHAT MUST YOU DO?

The first question involves what you need to do to satisfy your most basic needs. How do you provide yourself and your family with shelter, food, and clothing? These most basic needs are the most critical, especially to women raising a family. With your focus solely on these needs, you will generate an income and, in exchange, be fed and warm but may not find joy in your work or feel fulfilled. Almost all of us can hold a job that will provide for our most basic needs.

MIND – WHAT CAN YOU DO?

The second area involves what you can do, including all of the things that your mind is capable of. During your life you have built up a considerable set of skills and talents, and a lot of these can be used in your business or vocational life. It is possible to monetize this, but think of these talents and skills as the medium or the channel through which you can provide value to the world. You might have built up a skill set in writing or financial knowledge, which could translate into a career in journalism or financial planning. However, if you make a career decision without consideration for your heart and spirit, you may be operating from an opportunistic place that is unlikely to satisfy your inner desires.

HEART – WHAT GIVES YOU JOY?

The third area of consideration involves what you want to do – your heart area. What are you passionate about? What lights the fire in your belly? When you find the thing that you truly want to do, you will no longer focus on the effort of the task, and the work will simply flow through you. When you're in that creative space, you'll experience joy. Wouldn't it be wonderful to spend the majority of your time in that joyful place? When you are being yourself, and doing work that you enjoy, you'll find other people who share your interests. You'll be able to learn from them and be inspired by them. As that inspiration and passion grows you'll find a way to create a business that incorporates your heart area as well as incorporating your mind's skills and satisfying your bodily needs.

SPIRIT – WHAT GIVES YOU PURPOSE?

The fourth and final area is the spirit, and involves embracing the way that you contribute to the world. The people who have the greatest satisfaction in their lives are those who give the most. They are the artists who create pieces that change the world, or scientists who dedicate themselves to saving lives. They are the people who give freely and without restricting their best work. They provide value directly through their work, and they also provide inspiration to those around them. When you are contributing work of value, you'll be able to generate income to satisfy the body; you'll make good use of your talents and skills, and you'll operate in a place where your work is satisfying and brings you joy.

When you satisfy your spirit, and your sense of purpose and contribution, you'll be in alignment in all four areas and you will be living congruently.

YOUR VALUE IS IN YOUR VALUES

Natalie Archer, one of two creators of Bendelta, man-agement consulting firm with revenues in the mid-high single seven-figures, has just turned 35 years old. Even when Bendelta started 10 years ago, she had a vision of what the company could create.

I'm inherently strategic, and I love people, so the fact that we do strategy and leadership work means I inherently enjoy the work. But it's never been about that for me. It's about finding a context that inspires me, where I can thrive, and that context involved asking what the ideal business would be made of. That drove me down the entrepreneurial path. It also meant that I focused on hiring really well. It has meant that over time it is the team who has taken up the mantle of creating the ideal culture for our company.

Essentially I believe that you create the life that you expect. Things happen, and you come to understand that life might not pan out quite as idealized. But you can be a very strong influencer in terms of the kind of life that you experience. You can take total responsibility for how you feel, how happy you are, and whether or not you are doing things that feel aligned with your values. Those are the things I think we should be much more bold about – asking questions like "What could I change to make myself happier or more aligned to my values or desires at this point in time?" and then making changes to align our lives with the answer we give. I think this act of 'self-ish' courage serves us well.

FOR YOUR PURPOSE, TRY THE BE, DO, HAVE FRAMEWORK

If you're having difficulty finding your purpose with the Steve Pavlina model above, then there's another framework you can use to imagine – and create - your ideal life. This framework is the 'Be, Do, Have model'.

You decide who you would like to BE – the type of person you want to be in life, in business, and in your relationships. You also decide what you want to DO – what you would like to check off your bucket list over the next 5 years. And, of course, what you want to HAVE – what do you hope to have in your life, your relationships, what material possessions do you hope for, and what environment?

WHO DO YOU WANT TO BE

When you think about who you would like to BE, what springs to mind? It might be something non-specific, like an adventurer (which can exist in so many variations), or you can be as specific as you like. What particular qualities would you like to include in your ideal self? If you are an adventurer, would you rather have a swashbuckling adventure or a carefully planned one? Think about your relationships too. Do you want to be a successful entrepreneur, a loving spouse, an attentive parent, or a generous friend? Or perhaps all four?

WHAT DO YOU WANT TO DO

Consider what you want to DO with your life. There will probably be an overlap between who you would like to BE and what you would like to DO but they will not necessarily be the same thing. It comes down to identity. You might want to DO a marathon, but that doesn't mean that you have to BE a marathoner. When you're thinking about the things that you want to do you can include places to visit, goals that you want to accomplish and skills that you want to learn.

WHAT DO YOU WANT TO HAVE

As you move to what you want to HAVE, this is much more about material possessions. Remember, these are motivators. You can be as modest or as whimsical as you like - these are your desires after all – don't hold back! Some people recommend being single-minded in your desires, allowing you to concentrate on the most important goals and not be distracted. Others recommend building a long list of desires, around 150 bullet points, because it forces your mind to think of creative solutions to be able to achieve them all.

I'd encourage you to experiment on a small scale and see which approach resonates.

THE FEELING OF PURPOSE

A lot of the time when we think we are seeking a material goal, such as building a seven-figure business, what we are really craving are the feelings that we associate with that success. It might be a sense of security or a feeling of being recognized. It might even be the satisfaction of being able to make philanthropic contributions. It's a very rare person who wants to cuddle up to a pillow of cash. The money is merely a measure that tells us how effective we are.

When you think about your greater purpose, or when you talk about it, you might find that you overwhelmed by passion and emotion. Don't be discouraged, that's how you know that you're on the right path!

Laura Babeliowsky is a Dutch business coach who had her first $1 million turnover year in 2012.

"It's always about feeling the passion, the vision, and why you're passionate about it. For me, I want to help people be autonomous and to create their own income, independent of employers. That's my bigger why, and I'm very clear on this. It's such a strong passion that sometimes I feel that I could die, and my passion will still be here. I don't know where it comes from, but perhaps it has to do with my pain. That's why they say your passion has to be stronger than all the struggles, so that you can overcome them."

WHAT IS ENOUGH FOR YOU?

Just as important as knowing what drives you is recognising when you've arrived. What is your end goal? What is the point of the game?

Some women are so committed to their purpose, that it would be hard to imagine them leaving their business at all. Others are clear that their business has an end point, either a certain amount of money, or time, or impact on the world, and then they will be ready to move on to something else.

You might find that your end point changes over time. Being aware of what you want to achieve will help guide you.

Linda Simonsen created a $20 million turnover with Future People, a call center recruitment agency. After winning a high-ranking place in the prestigious BRW Fast 100 in 2006, she thought to herself:

It's time to get serious. This is a business I can make something of. I can build this business to attract investors – I'm going to grow it.

Shortly after that I was approached by a large brokerage about potential interest in buying my business. When I first set out, I thought the ultimate indicators of success would be if I built a business that someone else was willing to buy. I was pretty tired at this stage, working very long hours, and it was very stressful. The pressure, the stress of cash flow, where the next customer was going to come from, trying to get the right staff and assistance in place to make it work, all without a big budget.

I thought, in terms of a destination, that I was where I wanted to go, that I would sell the business. But when the offer came in, I looked at it and thought what if someone's willing to buy my business but doesn't know much about it. That's when I realized that I should be willing to back myself and try and take it to the next level. I decided to keep the business, to reinvest myself in it, and to take it to the next level, and that's exactly what I've done in the last five years.

DOWN TO BUSINESS - HOW TO (RE)CONNECT TO YOUR WHY

HOW TO FIND YOUR PURPOSE

If you're feeling that the business that you're currently in isn't correctly aligned with your purpose, then you might want to consider how to begin transitioning into one that is. I'm not advocating that you read this and immediately shut up shop. While for some people, that might be the right thing to do, for most people it's more appropriate to make the transition over a period of time.

Besides, the first thing to do before you pivot, is figure out what your purpose actually is.

During my own journey to find my purpose, and while helping my clients to find theirs - I use the following three activities. Feel free to work through each, or just follow the method that works best for you.

For each activity, you'll need a piece of paper or computer, an hour or so of uninterrupted time, and a willingness to engage in the process. If you prefer talking to writing, ask a friend to act as an interviewer and speak your answers out loud. Record the interview.

A) VALUES-DRIVEN PURPOSE

This is a series of exercises that will build on the answers from the previous exercises, so be sure to do them in order. If you haven't done any work on your purpose previously, then this will be a good way to get yourself into the right frame of mind to discover what is most important to you.

1. Choose three people you like and three you dislike. Summarize what you like and don't like about them.

2. Choose 10 values that you feel are most aligned to you. Put all the others to the side.

3. Look at which three of those values are the most important to you. For each of these three, write down what makes that value so important to you. How does it express itself in your life?

4. Write your life purpose as a statement, starting with "My Purpose in Life is..." keep in mind that your purpose is most powerful when it gives you a sense of contributing to something larger than yourself.

B) WRITE YOUR OWN EULOGY

Write your own eulogy – consider your ideal life. What would be said about you and your impact on the world?

Be aware that this exercise can be quite challenging and can bring up very powerful feelings. If it becomes too much, or starts to feel overwhelming, just stop. Put your pen down or turn off your computer and take a deep breath. We often find feelings of death quite confronting, and it may surprise you how strongly you feel.

You're going to write your own eulogy. Write it for your ideal self – the person you'd like to be when you let your imagination run wild. To be clear, this isn't what you think people will say about you now. This is what you want people to say about you.

This exercise is powerful because you will get a sense of your life from a perspective that you might not have considered before. If you want to be remembered as 'stylish' (for example), then you might realize that you need to pay more attention to your appearance. If you're a workaholic you might realize that you want to spend more time with family, or as an entrepreneur you might realize that you want to stop playing small and make a larger impact on the world.

Alternatively, you might finish this exercise and realise that you are actually on track, and already living the life you desire.

Either way, after this exercise you'll know more about yourself and what you want in your life.

If you're stuck or want more inspiration, here are some elements that are often included:

* What impact or contribution did you make?

* What were you passionate about? Was there a cause that you fought for or something that was an obsession for you?

* Who did you want to be when you were 12 years old?

* What lesson did you share with others such as your

kids, your friends, or people you just met?

* What elements of your life should be emphasized? Your relationship with your partner? With your kids? Your parents? Or your work or charity work?

* Did you have any great adventures or mishaps?

* What qualities set you apart?

* Did you have any personality flaws or strengths?

* What will be most missed about you?

When you've finished, read through it and make note of the things that surprised you. Write down the statement, "My purpose in life is..." and complete it with the new knowledge of what you want to see happen in your life.

C) CONSULT YOUR INTUITION / CONNECT WITH SOURCE

This activity is my personal favorite. This exercise allows you to access your intuition and connect with Source. It will generate a number of ideas that you might not generally allow yourself to have.

1. Take a blank sheet of paper or start up the computer – whichever is quicker to write on.

2. Write at the top, "What is my true purpose in life?"

3. Write an answer (any answer) that pops into your head. It doesn't have to be a complete sentence. Even a

short phrase or word is fine.

4. Repeat step three until you have the answer that
    makes you cry.

To some people, this will make sense. Others will think it's
crazy or even downright stupid. Even if you're sceptical, give
it a go, you might be surprised by what you discover. It might
take around 15–20 minutes to clear your mind and silence
your internal dialogue. The initial answers come from your
conscious mind and your memories. The real answer, when
it comes, will feel like it has been delivered from another
source entirely.

As you move through the process, you might find some
answers are similar. You might even write the same answers
over and over or go off on strange tangents. That's alright.
List whatever comes into your head. The only rule is to
keep writing.

At some point, somewhere between 50-100 answers, you'll
probably feel like quitting. Don't. You might feel the urge to
get up and do something else. This is normal. Push past the
resistance, and it will pass. Just keep writing.

You might also find that a few answers give you a tiny
surge of emotion, but not quite enough to make you cry;
highlight these as you go. You might want to come back to
them to generate new directions or lines of response. Each
of these emotive responses reflects a piece of the purpose,
but they're not complete in themselves.

It is important to do this alone and without interruptions.
It takes about 15–20 minutes to get into it, and each time
you are interrupted, it will take a few minutes to get back on
track, and the urge to get up and do something easier will be

stronger each time.

When you find your own unique answer to the question of why you're here, it will resonate deeply. The words will have a special energy to you, and you'll feel that whenever you read them, you might even find yourself overwhelmed with a flood of emotion.

CREATIVITY

Business isn't just a mechanistic process where you go through predetermined motions. It requires art and creativity. When you incorporate creative self-expression into your business, you pour yourself into the world.

In order to make sure that your well of creativity doesn't get depleted, you will need to connect to the source of your creativity and reenergize on a daily basis. Create a space for yourself where you can stop being pure output, and allow peace and creativity to flow into you. Allow yourself to re-engergize.

Linda Simonsen knows herself well now.

"I schedule time for creativity. You can get very caught up in the day-to-day, and my habits have had to change. I'm still trying to move through this, from where I was across everything in the business all the time, to actually creating time to think about the business and strategy and vision and innovation. So, I put time in my diary to do that. Otherwise, I find that there are weeks that go by and I think 'Oh! What about the creative piece?'"

As you give so much of yourself to the world, you'll need to find a way to replenish your own energy. There are a few things you should consider to ensure that you don't burn out. Set clear boundaries around you and your client work. If you are clear about what you are willing to share of yourself, you'll better protect the precious regenerative parts of you. You'll also want to protect your time, how much time you spend on your business, and how much do you spend on taking time out for yourself?

Another consideration is how you connect to the source of your creativity. The way that you start the day or nurture yourself throughout the day can contribute to your business success. The women interviewed in this book use different ways to access their creativity, but each has a consistent message about making time to just be, unrelated to work.

One aspect of nurturing your creativity is to be aware of your inner child. The inner child loves to play, to indulge, and to create without agenda. Focus on letting your inner child free throughout the day.

Carey Peters has co-created a health coaching business, Holistic MBA. She and her business partner have built this to $2.3 million despite being in different cities with different life interests.

I meditate and journal with spirit, source, whatever you feel is larger than you, and I do that regularly, and then I sing because it's what I love to do, and it makes me so happy that without it my workdays feel heavy.

My purpose is to be in service to whoever I'm in front of and to their soul's evolution. I believe that and whether it's performing and people get to access laughter, tears or be moved for my performance or whether it's coaching and people get to access possibilities for themselves they didn't see before, whatever it is, I'm in service to people and to their growth, personally and professionally.

Despite, or maybe because of, the time demands put on women who have built seven figure businesses, it's common to find a ritual that is used to center and ground them before they head out the door to the office.

Andrea Culligan is a Canadian who has ultimately landed in Sydney. She's built a number of businesses under the Unimail company with a combined turnover well into the seven figure range.

My husband and I wake up and literally ask each other 'Morning, what's the purpose for today?' My purpose today is to connect with you and other people that I'm meeting. That means being present, listening, communicating, and connecting.

I spend five minutes thinking about wonderful things in the world. It's a beautiful day, the trees are green, I've got a fluffy dog, and I get to laugh and have a roof over my head. I've got wonderful people that I get to work with everyday, great clients, I do good work, and the list goes on.

Then I spend five to ten minutes reading positive affirmations. They might be quotes or stories. But I always do this. Sometimes I even listen to them on my way to work, and then I write them down. I write down the things that I'm grateful for or things that are just wonderful in the world.

CHAPTER SUMMARY

* When your purpose and your business goals are aligned, you are able to continue through challenges, and more easily overcome fear and doubt.

* When you are connected with your business, it becomes a place of creativity and joy.

* Your values help to guide your purpose.

BONUS DOWNLOADS

Visit the exclusive resources section of the book at
www.oneextrazero.com/catapult/bonus

Take the downloadable assessment and discover how strong is your Catapult: A Woman's 7-Figure Business Quotient.

CHAPTER 2

TRIPLE YOUR VISION

When you start your business, you'll have a picture in your mind of what it looks like in its ideal state. Whatever that picture looks like to you, triple it.

When you first start a business, your main focus is survival. Then, after you've built a stable client base and have more confidence in what you are offering, you'll reach a plateau. Most business people stay there until they decide that what they offer is so valuable that they have to make the world aware of it.

If you take the vision for your business early on and triple it, you'll be able to move through those phases more quickly, and you'll start to think like a million dollar business owner much sooner, allowing you to recognize early on which skills you need to hone and which processes you need to build.

The next step is assertiveness. If you want something, you need to go out and get it. Success will not find you if you are your own best kept secret. So get comfortable with being visible. That means taking a stand (not just having a website), being able to get up in front of a group of people who may have more experience and better connections and being able to give them something of value. It means having the confidence to reach out to the journalist or blogger who has a connection to the audience you want. Putting yourself out there can be scary. Not everyone will like you – and that's tough to take sometimes. The ones who do like you need to see enough of you to fall in love.

A TYPICAL JOURNEY TO SEVEN FIGURES

When you're starting out, depending on your vision and what you want for your business, you might think that a seven figure business is out of your reach, or even that it is unnecessarily ambitious. If that's you, don't worry, you're not alone! But, what you'll most likely discover, once you reach the six figure revenue mark in your business, is that six figures isn't actually very much, especially if you have costs and taxes to pay.

And at the lower end of the six-figure range, you often end up very busy, with a good amount of work, but you might not have a great team to support you yet.

So you expand, accelerate, and push through, making it to $250,000. A quarter of a million is a lot, right? Well, it is, except you've had to hire an assistant and maybe a couple of other team members on a casual or part-time basis along the way. And you don't really have all of your systems in place yet, and you're now even busier than before because you haven't yet realized just how much other people should be doing for you. In fact, you're so busy, that you've started, every now and then, to drop the ball.

At the $250,000 mark, you decide again to expand. You hire the right team and make a commitment to invest seriously in your business, having faith that the business will succeed and the clients will come. You invest in more systems, get a customer relationship management tool, send out a newsletter and upgrade your order/shipping/billing system. All of these require a financial investment. In the meantime you're starting to participate in bigger events and you're considering holding events to increase your profile and visibility. You take a deep breath, jump in, and suddenly realize that you've doubled your business to $500,000 – half a million dollars!

At $500,000, you realize that you're still in demand, so you raise your prices – and not just by a little, in fact, you almost double them. You become more strategic with your time, aware of how important it is to focus your energy and yourself. And, just like that, you find that you are now at $1 million.

This is just one journey, and there are many paths to take along the way, but it's one that I hear often from my clients. There are also many challenges to face, but once you know your destination, even the biggest challenges become manageable.

SETTING A VISION

Setting a vision is about envisioning your preferred future. When you first create this vision, it can seem almost tangible. The vision should be what you imagine your ideal future to be. Of course, it's not here today, and it doesn't actually exist yet, so your imagination is a critical tool for this exercise.

If you have the ability to imagine what an outfit will look like before you put it on, or what your favorite dish will taste like, then you have enough imagination to be able to create your ideal vision of the future.

When you think about your business today, that's your reality. The mind-set, skills and relationships that created your business reality are the mind-sets, skills and relationships of yesterday.

If you want your business to continue to grow and expand, you will need to create a new mind-set, learn new skills, and foster new relationships to drive you forward.

When you give yourself time to envision about what you want your business to look in the future, you allow the details of today – and yesterday - to dissipate. You stop being distracted by the real challenges of hitting your monthly milestones, or the difficulties you encounter with members of your team, or even the stresses of today's to-do list.

Setting a vision puts you in an expansive frame of mind and allows you to think creatively about where you want to take your business. Looking forward allows you to connect to a future that is possible beyond your current reality and helps you to consider what you want your future reality to look like.

If you want your business to reach seven figures, you will almost definitely need to have a stronger impact than you do today. You will need to reach more people, and touch more lives.

Laura Babeliowsky found that she could set a vision, and be able to reach it, just because she decided it was possible.

I learned you can imagine a higher vision, and I developed the self-confidence to make this higher vision come to life. Originally, I was always insecure. 'Can I really do this? I don't believe it'.

Now I know that you can do it just because you want to. Because you decide to do it. That's the biggest decision that you can make. Your vision comes about because you decide that it should.

ALLOW YOUR PURPOSE TO DRIVE YOUR VISION

Once you have created your purpose, you need to connect it to your vision. Then you need to connect your purpose to a business model, paying special attention to who you serve, what problems you solve, and the solutions that you offer.

Natalie Archer of Bendelta is clear on her vision. As well as creating a business that impacts one million people directly (and one billion indirectly), she has been an active board member of World Vision NZ for the past 10 years.

I remember sitting down at the Paddington Inn with my future business partner, thinking about why we should set up our own business and what the name would be. We wanted to set up a business that did great things – that could compete with the best of them but where we didn't have to compromise our values and beliefs in what a working environment could look, feel and be like. So we came up with the name on a coaster at the bar – Bendelta – which was a sort of melding of the Latin word Bene meaning well or positive, and the Greek word Delta meaning change. So Bendelta was born a company that would stand for positive change.

After the first two and half years, we reached an interesting juncture. We were earning good money and had incredible flexibility, but re-examining the reason we started business in the first place. We'd wanted to build something that was demonstrative of positive change in terms of impacting human potential and defining business in a way that we actually thought was sustainable.

We decided to go back to the reason we started. So we came up with something called the Bendelta Code, which is our set of values. The first rule is "There are no rules (if we've hired you, it's because we trust you. Use your best judgement)," through to "We think big", "We collaborate", "We value each person for themselves (except where it's funny)". The last one is tongue in cheek and is a reminder that amongst all of the humanity is a desire to have a laugh and not take ourselves too seriously. Going hand in hand with the Bendelta Code is our Vision – 1 million 1 billion, which is our desire to directly impact 1 million people to realise their positive potential and 1 billion people indirectly through the work we do.

THE PROBLEM WITH AN UNCLEAR VISION

If you don't have an image of what our vision is, you can't know where you're going. A vision allows you to feel that you're moving toward something that is substantially different from where you are now, which motivates change and propels you forward.

Without a strong vision of your preferred future, it's easy to get stuck in the daily grind of your current work situation. The pressures of managing our lives effectively can be relentless. No matter where you are on your entrepreneurial journey, you'll find that there are challenges.

All of your challenges can be overcome. But if you look at your challenges too simply you will be limiting the potential of your solution. If you are consistently seeking solutions for individual problems instead of looking at the broader context of your business, each problem will start to seem insurmountable.

If instead, you expand your creative vision so that you are consistently asking yourself, "How do I reach the place that I want to get to?" then the problem that seemed so insurmountable will become just one more step along the path on the way to your destination.

Bestselling author Steven Covey describes this as, "Begin with the end in mind." Everything that comes to be has two elements. The first time it happens, it happens inside the head; it is just imagined. The second time something happens, it happens in the physical world. This means that you want to be very clear about what you want to develop.

HAVE A CLEAR PICTURE OF YOUR FUTURE, THEN TRIPLE IT

I want to give you a challenge.

Once you've carefully built your vision for your business, look at it, hold it in your imagination and notice how you feel when you consider it. It will feel good, satisfying even. You're sitting back, eyes closed, and you're thinking, "If my business and my life looked like that, it would be ideal. Perfect. Just really marvelous."

Now, triple that vision.

How would your vision look if you were serving three times the number of people? Or if you had three times the number of support staff on your team? If your business had three times the revenue? What about if you were three times as influential, downloaded, or purchased? If you appeared as a guest on TV shows that had three times the audience? Or what if you ran your own TV show? What if you were living in your dream home that cost three times as much?

This exercise forces you to look beyond your own inbuilt limitations and makes you see who you could become if you weren't limited by your own imagination. It allows you to push at the boundaries of what you think you are capable of and takes you that little bit further. Tripling it allows you transform yourself, beyond your humble visions and shows you what is truly possible.

If your new vision – the tripled one - makes your fingers tingle, and your heart race, then maybe that's what you should have been envisioning all along!

Andrea Culligan, with a branding business already well into seven figures, recommends getting clearer on a bigger vision earlier on.

If I went back in time, I would give my younger self this advice: I would tell her to focus, focus on one thing at a time, and go bigger. Just go as big as you possibly can. Think bigger; have a bigger vision; triple your vision and just explore everything around it. Explore your competitors and the associations; find out what your customers want; find out what your audience wants and just focus on those things; just do that. And, all those other things that you're really not great at, get someone else to do them.

YOU DON'T NEED TO KNOW THE STEPS TO GET TO THE VISION

Business owners and entrepreneurs often have a vision that is bigger than the business they are actively planning for.

There's a gap between where they want to take their business, and the perfect day that they imagine for themselves. One of the most powerful exercises I do with my clients is to ask them to look at how much revenue or profit they want their business to be bringing in over the next year or 5 years, compared with what their ideal day looks like. Quite often there's a sizeable gap between the lifestyle that they want and the goals that they have set for the business.

The path to get to your vision doesn't have to be perfectly clear, as long as you know where you are heading. There's a beautiful story about the value of knowing your destination even if you don't know the actual path.

Let's say you need to go on a car drive from Sydney to Melbourne, a trip of just under 1,000km (600 miles). You also need to do it at night. You know the destination, but you don't have a GPS or a map, just a general idea that you need to head south and drive for a while. By turning on your headlights, you're able to see 100 meters or so ahead of you. You see some signs along the way and you follow them when you see them. You might ask for directions or even confirm that you're heading in the right direction with people you meet on the way. And, without having a road map that spells out every twist and turn, you eventually get there.

Kendall SummerHawk believes that the quickest way to for businesses to catapult themselves to seven figures is to just imagine that they are already there and to do the things that a million dollar business owner would do. Kendall attributes this mindset as accelerating her business from $100,000 to $1 million in less than two years.

I tell people to focus on being a million dollar business owner. That's the one mindset that pulled me forward the fastest. When you start having to ask yourself, "As a million dollar business owner, what would I do in this situation?", you start making decisions from where you want to be, not from where you've come from.

WHAT'S YOUR END POINT?

Where do you want to end up with your business? When you consider your vision of your ideal day, is your business still with you, or have you let it go? Do you have a goal in mind that will let you know that you've made it? What's your number? At some point, you're going to want to exit your business, or at least have the choice to. It might be that you plan to build it up to a saleable asset to give yourself a great retirement. Or maybe you'll bring in some young blood and stay on as a grand matriarch overseeing the operations even when they have to wheel you out on to the terrace for your afternoon gin and tonic. Or perhaps you want some young blood to do a management buy-out. Or you might just take it public.

Whatever it is, you need to have a clear end point in mind. When you get there, you will experience incredible pride, joy and satisfaction, and you'll also be ready for the next phase in life.

Natalie Archer is in the process of significantly changing pace.

I'm going to scale back next year and make more room for other things. I love what I do, and I would keep doing it 'round the clock. It just pulls me in, and I find it inherently satisfying, rewarding, and exciting. But I want a balanced life, a family, a relationship, love, and hopefully children. Those things are really important to me, so I'm simply going to create the space.

I'm going to learn a musical instrument. I'm going to learn how to dance better than I do because I think that's a really cool, creative, feminine thing. I know it will make me a better leader. I'll be 35 in December, and it's a really important decision that I need to make. I set the business up to be able to have the best of both worlds. I think back to when I listened to the QC, and I dropped out of law because that was a life completely dominated by a career. I wanted to have an amazing career, but I wanted to be able to shape it in my own way. I have a wonderful life with lots of different elements to it, and now I find myself 10 years into the business, having loved it and still loving it, and I want to continue to love it. But I'm not honoring the key reason for my choice in the first place, which was to have it all.

It's good to know what your end point is, but it's even more important to recognize when the end-point changes.

Linda Simonsen really wanted to build a business that would list on the stock exchange, but the surprise arrival of a baby boy shifted those plans. The arrival of Lucas created a shift in the business plans and opened an awareness to the importance of emotional intelligence.

Initially the business was about survival, and then it was about making money and creating financial security. Now it's about building a great culture and working with clients that are like-minded, so I feel like I'm fulfilling my true purpose.

I've definitely softened from the hardnosed businesswoman wanting to grow a $100 million dollar business that would list on the stock exchange to wanting to do good work and invest in valuable relationships and try to be there for my son, Lucas.

I'm actually his maternal aunt, and when he was born in 2009, my sister wasn't able to care for him, so I cut his cord and took him home from the hospital, and he's been with me ever since.

We were coming off the GFC; I had this bad debt [from a client who went under]. Life was not good, and suddenly I had this little baby to care for who was quite sick. I'd always thought, "I'll get to having kids later," and by this stage I was single. I hired a nanny to help and tried to juggle this tiny baby and the business at the same time. It was tough, but it shaped me considerably, and it made me understand what is really important in life. Lucas is the best thing that ever happened to me, and he's given me a new appreciation for relationships.

DOWN TO BUSINESS – MAKING YOUR VISION TANGIBLE

STORY TELLING

Once you're clear on your vision, turn it into a story.

If you go to a talk or a conference, you will forget most of the facts and figures quickly. You might remember some of the pictures that they show, or the presenter's tone or mannerisms as they gave their presentation. There's something very human about the way that we remember visual details.

You will however, almost certainly remember a story. We are hard-wired to remember stories. We have learned them while sitting around campfires. They have become ways for information to reliably travel from one city to another, even after months of travel.

We have archetypes written into our psyche. Even without a deep knowledge of classical literature theory, we can all describe the hero and the villain of the story. We know who is the fool and who is the sage. These archetypes allow us to recognize the characters that shape and define the story and make it easier to grab hold of the twists and turns.

A PRESENTATION CONVEYS FACTS AND IS FORGOTTEN

You'll have seen this yourself if you've spent any amount of time listening to formal presentations or keynote addresses.

There will be the speaker who stands up and gives you the five characteristics of leadership, ways to develop leadership, and tools and techniques to get you started. The characteristics are goal setting, determination, resilience, perseverance, and building a team. One PowerPoint slide for each with bullet points underneath. By the time the speaker has finished, all you can remember is that it's time for lunch.

A GREAT STORY EVOKES EMOTION

Then there will be the athlete who tells the story about how, at the age of 16, when she was a bit of a loner, she was confronted by her coach about whether she really wanted to win or not, and she decided to become the best. She had some early wins, and then some setbacks, like the time she was in a car accident and broke her leg in three places. The setbacks were so difficult that she almost gave up. She wanted to give up. She even tried to give up, but she found that she couldn't leave her dream behind so she clawed her way back, competing first at the local, then state, and finally the national level. It wasn't an easy path, but she concentrated on the big picture, as well as the tiny steps, getting away faster at the start, turning sharper on the bends, and accelerating through the finish. Increment by increment, she improved and climbed back up the ladder. She didn't worry about her competition or where they ranked against her. She just knew she wanted to be the best she could be.

She learned goal setting, determination, resilience, perseverance, and built a support team. And finally, there she was at the international level, ready to compete... and unlike the first version of the leadership presentation, you have leaned forward, engaged in the story, and now want to know what happens, right?

(She wins, of course, because it's a story.)

TELL A STORY THAT COMMUNICATES YOUR VISION

Stories transform our understanding of the world, so as you develop your vision, share it with the people who will benefit from it (your customers), as well as those who will help you make it happen (your team). When your business starts out, you need to be focused on where your marketing budget goes. It is so easy for your message to be diluted and you need to focus on engaging with the right people and having the right conversations.

I spent some time doing a creative writing course at a writing center in Sydney's East with the remarkable Roland Fishman. My goal wasn't to have a finished novel, but I very much wanted to understand the narrative process. The arc of a story and the development of a main character are crucial for a quality story.

So, as you think about your story, ask yourself why you are in business, and why people should support your business. You want to be telling a story about yourself that engages and inspires.

Valerie Khoo has a wonderful book, Power Stories: The 8 Stories You Must Tell to Build an Epic Business." One of the stories is about developing your leadership message. In that leadership chapter, she describes how the power of story-telling motivates and inspires and becomes a beacon that can unite people behind a movement or a product that they believe in. Through your story, you'll need to show people who you are and determine exactly what is different about your business or organisation. Why should people support or believe in your ability to deliver?

You'll also need to inspire people to take action. What is your call to action? How can people be a part of your mission? Beyond your desire to serve this individual client, is there a broader mission that you want to share? This might be the purpose you developed in Chapter 1. Is there a way to share this story about how you came to be in the business, which leads back into your greater mission of the good that you want to do in the world?

Building a successful business means that you know who your ideal clients are and what they want. People only really recognize a message when it is speaking directly to them.

The days of having a captive audience ready to consume a broadcast message are gone. We value our independence, and we want language that shows recognition of our unique situation and insight into our problems.

BUILD YOUR BRAND, GET ATTENTION AND BE POLARIZING

Building your brand can be as intentional or unintentional as you like, but you need to have a brand in the market. The market is so crowded, and clients and consumers are so time poor, that very few people will have the time, interest, or resources to really go on a quest to understand you.

It's hard to build a brand if nothing stands out. Branding is just a shorthand way of saying what you stand for so that people can recognize you. Women service professionals need to be recognized by the things that they do and stand for.

Within your chosen sphere, you'll want something that lets you build an element of celebrity (i.e. known for something). Getting business is all about being top of mind with your clients. If you are drowning in the sea of mediocrity, then you'll struggle to be anywhere close to being remembered, let alone top of mind.

The enduring way to be remembered is to be at the top of your field for excellence and to have views that are expressed clearly as a way for the industry and your clients to move forward.

Ariel Hyatt has a seven figure social media business based out of New York, working initially with the music industry and now increasingly with female entrepreneurs who have a message to get out. At the beginning, it was all pure and creative bootstrapping.

I had to get creative because I was working for independent and emerging artists and bands; they didn't have a lot of money. There was a giant paper warehouse a couple of miles from my house, and they had every type of paper and paper clip. I spent hours putting the bands' press kits together, matching the different colors, and really thinking about the fonts that the stuff would be printed on. Every client had his or her own very specific branded look that I worked really hard to create.

I also had to figure out how to get those envelopes opened by the media, I got a catalogue of cheap toys and party favors. I ordered thousands of little toys, everything from little plastic spiders to cute glow-in-the-dark rings. I got stickers made up which said, "Toy Surprise Inside", just like Cracker Jack, and I put a little toy inside every envelope that went out.

I tried to be the little PR firm that people would talk about. And I also made a branding choice to name the company after myself. I called it Ariel Publicity and I had fun with the logo, which was a little caricature of me.

KNOW WHO YOUR IDEAL CLIENTS ARE

When you are very clear about your vision, your ideal client will understand your message instantly, so you need to find a way to identify and reach that client.

This is critical to your success.

You'll find that the number of people who might be possibly interested in your service will be far greater than the number of people with whom you can effectively build trust and credibility. This is particularly true when you are just starting out.

WHY IS IT IMPORTANT?

There are a couple of reasons. First, it helps you to understand them properly. If you don't know what problems your ideal client has, then your solution is not going to be as specialized and specific as it needs to be. Without a specialized solution you aren't going to be able to charge premium rates. Think about your medical general practitioner and your specialist. You are willing to pay the specialist five times more, because your unique problem is important to you and you want it fixed.

Second, knowing who your ideal client is helps you find them and be in front of them more easily. If you are able to serve people deeply, then you'll find that your marketing efforts are better focused on a narrow and deep segment. Marketing for services is built on reputation and trust, and both of these take time to develop. If you have to develop reputation and trust across too broad a swathe of the population, you'll be exhausted before you get going.

Your degree of specialization will also depend on your price point. If you are working on contracts that are upwards of $500,000 each, then you'll want very deep relationships with a few buyers. On the other hand, if you are working with clients who spend less than $1,000 annually, then you'll want to find a cost-effective way of reaching more clients (or increasing the annual spend).

THE TRUE BUYER BUYS YOUR VISION

Getting your vision to become reality will be difficult if you can't find people who are willing to invest in your services and to help your business grow.

Finding the true buyer is important for those who sell to businesses. If you want to have an impact on the world, you need to be talking to the people who are willing, ready, and able to buy.

For any purchase, there is always a decision-maker. Somebody owns the decision to spend the money. An entrepreneurial organization often has the founder as the key decision maker, with a few influencers. A large corporation will often have a greater degree of complexity in those who influence buying decisions either directly or indirectly, but there will still be someone who has ownership of that budget and decides how to spend it.

Corporate departments are under an obligation to spend their budgeted money, otherwise they risk losing their allocation in the next budget. This applies to marketing costs just as much as training costs. Anyone who has worked in corporate will remember the annual flurry to allocate unspent money in the budget. I've even heard tales of organizations spending money on projects that were poorly defined and sometimes never executed with suppliers, just to get the money out of the system and have the budget replenished the following year.

YOUR TIME IS IMPORTANT WHEN YOU NEED TO SHARE YOUR VISION

You need to think strategically about how you spend your time. You don't want to waste your business time talking to someone who isn't authorized to make a purchase, or someone who is a lovely person but doesn't have the money to invest in your product or service.

As a woman who has an incredible service to give to the world, you have an obligation to build business relationships, not with everyone, but with the people who will give your gift an opportunity to flourish.

Tools such as LinkedIn are powerful for seeing through the veil of corporate organization charts and government layers and identifying the world of quasi-governmental statutory bodies.

But it's really not that useful unless you can figure out who the true buyer is. You need to be able to find the person who can authorize the spend. Generally, this is NOT the HR director. The HR department is often just the coordinator of other departments' training budgets. They might be instructed to come up with a training solution, or, even more specifically, to have a shortlist of three proposals that will help the team, but they don't always have visibility on the measure that is trying to be improved, the detail behind what drove the request for training in the first place.

Experts in sales use a series of qualifying questions to ensure that they're talking to the right people. When you call for the appointment, be sure to ask for the person by responsibility, not name. And then, when confirming the appointment, always double check.

Some take it one step further in asking specific questions. They will want to know whose budget the purchase will hit. They ask what measures need to be improved by this program or service. You only want to get in front of the person who knows the answers to those questions; otherwise you lessen your ability to get your message out, and your ability to sell subsequent programs.

If you can, take a simple black and white view of your business relationships. Build relationships with people who can make buying decisions. Don't be dismissive of those who can't, but don't invest your precious time.

If you've been struggling to get your proposals across the line with an organization, ask yourself if you're really speaking to the right person.

If you know that you have a vision that needs to be brought to life through your business, then you need to be able to find the people who can help you do that.

CHAPTER SUMMARY

* Knowing your vision for yourself and your business is critical to knowing where you want to go. Once you have the vision, the journey reveals itself. It's not possible to know all the steps when you first set out.

* Challenge yourself to triple your vision early on.

* Use stories to convey your vision.

* The number of people who are interested in what you do is greater than you realize, but you must focus on reaching them. Know your ideal clients, their problems, and your solution inside out and better than they themselves do, so you can find them and talk to them effectively.

BONUS DOWNLOADS

Visit the exclusive resources section of the book at
www.oneextrazero.com/catapult/bonus

Take the downloadable assessment and discover how strong is your Catapult: A Woman's 7-Figure Business Quotient.

Complete your own Blueprint for Describing What You Do

Complete your Storytelling Template

CHAPTER 3

COMMIT TO YOUR SUCCESS

"If you want to be successful, you have to take 100% responsibility for everything you experience in your life. This includes the level of your achievements, the results that you produce, the quality of your relationships, the state of your health and physical fitness, your income, your debts, your feelings, everything!"
—Jack Canfield

When you create a business, you'll quickly discover that no one cares about it more than you do. Your business needs you as much as a newborn does. At the beginning, and for quite some time, you'll be the only one that is able to generate any momentum. If you stop showing up, then the business will falter and fail. Total responsibility means that if your business needs more customers, you are responsible for making sure your business gets more clients. If your business needs a new system, you will have to somehow bring that on board; even if you don't do the work yourself, you have the ultimate responsibility to put the resources in place to make it happen. And when a crisis comes, then you will be the one to put out the fire and to make sure there are no embers left burning.

Your employees, your family, and even your friends won't fully understand the importance of keeping your business alive and thriving. There will be so many opportunities to give up. Challenges are par for the course; every business has them, and every business owner needs to overcome them.

BUILDING A BUSINESS TAKES COMMITMENT

You need to know why you're doing it and what your ultimate goal is. Knowing your purpose gives you the power that will propel you forward when you falter or get stuck. The unwavering belief that what you are doing is needed and valuable in the world is critical.

How badly do you want to have success in your business and your life? The real reason that most people don't have successful businesses is because they don't really want it, or didn't make it a true priority. They think that they would have to give up part of themselves, that they would have to change.

COMMITTING HAS REWARDS

The women in this book have revealed that they have changed as their businesses grew. But, each of them found that change to be overwhelmingly positive. They like who they have become. These women have transformed in the process of building their businesses. They have become more assertive with clearer boundaries, they are more passionate about what is important to them, and they know that spending time with their loved ones gives them time to connect and recharge.

Andrea Culligan describes her relationship with perseverance and her understanding that challenging situations have forged the woman that she is today.

I have had some really tough times over the last few years. One of our business partners took us through a lawsuit that went all the way to the high court, which, thankfully, we won. It was like a divorce, it was so emotionally taxing. We lost a lot of market share to our competitor, which I had to face, and that was personally quite confronting. However, I look at all of those things with the most immense gratitude.

Often, in difficult times, people who are working for others will say 'Oh! You have a choice, you know. It's your choice,' and that statement really makes me mad. People somehow think that the choices you make will always be easy and will always be fun. Choices aren't always fun; sometimes choices are hard, and sometimes choices mean you've got to be involved in things you'd rather not be. But that's the difference between running your own business and working for someone else. When you work for someone else, you do have a choice. If you really hate something, you can just walk away. It's up to you. But if you're really prepared to give it your all, to go through thick and thin, prepared to fail or succeed, and you absolutely know you'll go

to the nth degree, then you have to make choices that will not
always be nice. And the people who are prepared to walk away
when things get that tough, they will never understand that.
They will never understand what that feels like because they
are just driven by different things.

YOU CHOOSE YOUR LEVEL OF SUCCESS

You have chosen the life you have now. It sounds very
black and white, doesn't it?

Everything in your life right now, good and bad, is there
because you have allowed it to happen.

The same principle applies when it comes to your business.

You choose how many customers you have, what services
you provide, and how much revenue you make. You choose
whether you do everything, or whether you leverage your
time through hiring a team. You choose how much time you
invest in learning about sales and marketing and about managing your precious commodity of time.

IT'S NOT OK FOR THIS NOT TO WORK

Many of the women featured in this book have had a
pivotal moment. Some call it rock bottom, others call it the
breakdown before the breakthrough. The moment when
nothing is going well, when all you can see in front of you is
despair and loss. It's a 4 a.m. moment when you're wondering
if it will ever be better than it is now, wondering where your
next customer will come from, and questioning if you have
the strength to look at your dismal cash flow again. You go
through each of your options again and realize that you've

exhausted them all. Nothing has worked, and you seriously wonder if anything ever will.

Rock bottom is filled with panic and despair. There is no emotional rope to cling onto, and sometimes it's not even clear whether you should continue to struggle, or just surrender.

The good news is that when you hit rock bottom it's solid. The bad news is that it's not a place you want to be; it's miles below where you want to be. At that moment, you have to make a decision. Are you so relieved that you have finally finished falling that you resign yourself to staying at that level? Or is it time to get back up?

THE DECISION TO COMMIT OFTEN COMES AT ROCK BOTTOM

It is during those moments of despair that you need to say "This is going to work." That it's going to be a success because you're destined for a life that is better than this. It might be a spiritual epiphany; it might be the grim grit of determination that gives you strength and direction. Whatever it is, take hold and don't let go!

Carey Peters had a moment where she vowed that things would be different.

There was a time about four years ago when I was sitting on the hardwood floor of my office crying my eyes out because I had $14,000 in my bank account, no savings, no retirement, no sense of financial freedom, and I was 34 years old. I remember thinking, 'This is not right.' In that moment, I made the *decision that I was never going to be in that financial position again AND that I was going to make a living doing what I loved. I wanted to have a business where I could work from anywhere in the world, especially from home. It was rock bottom from my perspective, but anyone looking in from the outside would say, 'That's crazy. You have people buying products from you. You have people begging you; they want to hire you. What's the deal? Just ask them to be your client!'*

When I made that decision to become serious, I did three things. I invested in a coach training program for business and marketing. I wanted to have the education in addition to my own expertise. Next, I invested in a mind-set coach because I knew that I was the source of the problem. I didn't know much, but I knew that I was the one creating these problems, and that I was the one who was not seeing opportunities and didn't have confidence in myself. After those investments, the third thing I did was to finally make an offer to my list for a coaching program, and, literally, in 30 days, made $40,000.

Many successful entrepreneurs have had a rock bottom moment. Then they had a vision of themselves rising up and overcoming adversity. That sense of spirit cannot be crushed by failure.

If you've been beaten down, you need to make peace with yourself, and be aware that not every challenge is easy to climb over, but if you give yourself enough time, and equip yourself with enough resources, eventually you will be able to make it to the other side.

Sometimes it feels like divine intervention. You get to a place where it seems that you can't go on, and so, in quiet desperation, you make a bargain with the universe.

Leela Cosgrove, who has built a seven-figure Internet marketing and sales business, did just this. Her rock bottom was a place that she decided she just didn't want to stay in any longer.

In 2004, I was literally supporting myself, my now ex-husband and two sisters on $100 a day. I was constantly asking myself what I could do to make money. I've always been very good with words, so I started looking online for freelance writing work. I came across a website called guru.com. There was not a lot of Australian work on Guru in those days, but I put my name and details on there and set myself up to receive weekly work notifications and heard nothing ... for a year.

In 2005, I went through a very nasty divorce, and I had gone to see my mother in Bangalow. One night, looking out over beautiful Byron Bay, I got really fed up. I put my foot down and said, 'I'm sick of this ... so here's my deal, Universe. You're going to start putting opportunities in front of me, and I guarantee you, I am going to do everything it takes to be worthy of them.' I called this my demandifesto...

In the morning, less than 12 hours later, I received an email for an admin position, which immediately evolved into a writing job. I started working for the Managing Director of the Jay Abraham Company in Australia. Jay Abraham is the marketing genius who worked with companies like Baskin 'n' Robbins and Lockheed Martin. He is the guy behind the Tony Robbins' infomercials. He's one of the greatest marketing minds in the last 80 years. I wrote information products and marketing

material for Jay Abraham, and then began doing some of the
marketing work for Robbins' events in Australia. And it all
started less than 12 hours after my demandifesto.

Have you ever wondered if you have it in you to rise up from a position where you feel defeated? Here's the thing: if you can imagine it, you can do it. It might not happen immediately and it might not be easy, and you have to be willing to throw everything you have at it in order to gain that momentum and catapult yourself forward.

THE COMMITMENT JOURNEY

How to succeed? Try hard enough.
—Malcolm Forbes

The first 12–36 months of any new business are often called the Journey of Faith. Clients aren't always plentiful. Cash flow might be uncertain and erratic, and unless you are already a successful serial entrepreneur, then the whole process is likely to be an enormously steep learning curve.

Not every successful entrepreneur or business owner needs to have had a rock bottom experience. There are a couple of women who found this first period of time relatively easy and the work plentiful. They still weren't experts at running a business. There was still a great deal to learn about leadership, leverage, and time. However, it was more a matter of running to keep up. It could be intense, but rewarding.

In those cases, the momentum still came from inside, and they were looking at creating a business with the best of something – the best customer service, the best customer satisfaction. They were very aware of what they were creating.

Sophie Bartho, an Australian who has since sold her seven-figure creative design business, attributes her early success to being both lucky and good at what she was offering the market.

My business was SBA Designs, and I wanted to provide design services to a broad sector of the industry. Back then, my peers were focusing on specializing; so you did either packaging design, or you did corporate design. I wanted to be constantly challenged, and I found by mixing the corporate with the fast moving consumer goods packaging work kept me more inspired, more creative, more agile.

My first customer was a PR firm, and I was working for one of their clients on creating a corporate identity. I was very fortunate in that it was a high quality product. There was mutual respect between me and the PR firm, and the PR firm and their client, so I had direct access to their client. It was a very good three-way relationship.

Within the first six months, I had my first big break. Someone else in the industry contacted me about a job for Coco Cola Amatil. It was a big job with a short turnaround, and I said 'Yes'. That was a big turning point because I delivered, and then more work came from Coke. Having a brand like that in your portfolio opens doors. And it happened again with another big corporate client. Together, they became two of my biggest clients for probably 15 years.

Others found the beginnings the hardest. Many women started businesses trading on their area of expertise and quickly found that they knew nothing about marketing themselves, or promoting themselves in a way that felt authentic and honorable. As a result, their sales efforts were, let's say, patchy.

These situations can help build commitment and confidence quickly. When you're in a place where you don't know what you're doing, and the money isn't flowing, then you enter survival mode, where you have to figure out how to make it work.

Once you figure out what you need to do, then you'll have a greater sense of confidence in your own ability and desire to succeed.

Kendall SummerHawk figuratively burned her bridges, there was now only one way forward, and she got down to work.

My first year in business was miserable. I was doing all the things wrong, I was doing all the things that I now teach people not to do. I wasted a lot of time and money having get-to-know you lunches and coffees; I don't even drink coffee. I didn't have any idea how to ask for the sale. I didn't know how much to charge. I didn't have any idea how to translate or connect the dots between the processes that I knew how to do and how that will actually benefit people. So I felt very lost for close to a year. I went to my mom everyday crying and say, 'I don't know what I'm doing'. I was rapidly running out of money, the man I was married to at the time was mostly out of work and we were on a path to divorce so that was not a joyful supportive environment. There came a day something needed to shift.

I pulled out my résumé because I thought I might have to go out and get a job, and I felt like I was going to throw up. I felt like such an utter failure. I just said to myself, 'I can't do that, I just cannot do that.' And so I threw the résumé away, and I deleted the file from my computer. And I got busy taking some teleseminars on marketing; I really loved what I learned and I put it into action right away and I kind of discovered by accident that I had a knack for marketing. That was August 2000.

I just woke up one day and said okay, I'm going to be a coach. So I called three people that day, and invited them to a complimentary coaching session with me; I said I want you to get to know me so that you feel comfortable referring me. And all three hired me.

TOTAL RESPONSIBILITY

Taking total responsibility means figuring out what's going wrong and developing a plan to fix it. You might need to look deeper than the business, though. You might need to do some work on you in order to find your solution.

The scope of responsibility can seem enormous, but it is an enormous opportunity as well.

Take an honest look at yourself. Is your mindset holding you back? Do you believe, deep down, that you deserve to have a successful business? Do you believe it's even possible? These are not easy questions to answer, and the answers will change depending on the results of your day, your environment, and your energy levels. That's why faith in your vision is so important!

Then, take a look at your business. What's working? What's not working? Are your customers delighted with your offerings? Customer service is an area that is sorely lacking and businesses can limp along with mediocre performance, never achieving their potential. You need to be able to look at the business with a diagnostic eye. What processes need to be tightened? If you don't have enough customers, then it's sales and marketing. If you don't have good repeat or referral business, then it might be the product or service itself. And if your cash is all over the place, then there are financial controls that can help tighten this up. If your area of specialty lies outside of these areas, find someone who can help and be brave enough to learn what's going on.

Linda Simonsen would have found it easier to just give up, but had such a belief in herself and in her vision, that she always decided to keep on going, no matter what. Her call center recruitment business now sits at $20 million turnover.

In the early stages, it was just one day at a time, one customer at a time, and as we got customers, I remember doing crazy things. I'd been to the bank and presented a business plan. I was quite a high-income earner before I started the company, and the bank had been throwing credit cards and all sorts of unsecured loans at me until I wanted to start a business. They made me jump through a lot of hoops, and, even though my business plan was very solid, they wouldn't give me any funding because I didn't have any property.

Looking back, I think I was a little bit crazy to start a recruitment business without a lot of money because the one thing you learn in recruitment is cash flow is everything. When you place temporary staff with clients and call centers have large work forces, you need to pay them, but you might not get paid for 30 or even 45 days.

I applied for every credit card I could get, to the sum of $70,000 worth of credit on credit card. Making payroll meant juggling cash advances on my credit cards to pay the temps without trying to sound desperate when asking clients to pay. No one really understood, and when I was down to my last $200, I thought, 'What comes next?'

There's a necessary element of determination when planning and doing the numbers. In theory, if you're good at what you do, then the numbers will reflect that. I had to develop real discipline regarding how many prospective customers I needed to talk to, and also I was small. I had to remember that every 'no' was one step closer to the next 'yes'. My strategy was very much – deliver really amazing service and try to build the business based on referrals, and that's exactly how we grew.

TOTAL RESPONSIBILITY FOR YOUR LEADERSHIP

You also need to be the CEO; the true leader of the business. You are responsible for the direction of the business and the strategic plays that you put in place to get there. Who are your key clients? What are your main product offerings? If it's not working, is there something else that might be working better? You cannot have any tolerance for products or services that fail to perform.

As the leader, you are responsible for your team, the culture, and the time. Leadership is not about making friends. If a team member isn't performing you don't have to keep him or her in the business. Your responsibility is to your business.

Sophie Bartho talks about learning this on the job.

My big shift was moving from being colleague to boss or leader of the organization. As a leader, there are some hard decisions you have to make and communicate. I found it very hard to sit down with a staff member and do a performance review or address an issue, and then, two hours later, go out to the pub with them.

I remember my dad saying to me, 'Sophie, they want you to be their leader, not their friend. Go to the pub, have one drink, and then go. Let them get on with having a good time.' It was as if someone finally gave me permission. I didn't have to stay and socialize with them in addition to leading the organization. I think you need to clarify the role you play by asking, 'what is the most important role I've got here.'

TOTAL RESPONSIBILITY FOR YOUR SKILLS

You also need to take responsibility for your own skills and talents. Your vision will be meaningless if you don't take responsibility for the practical elements of getting out there and developing your talents. If it takes 10,000 hours to becoming an expert, then having the ability to practice your skills is a requirement for your success.

Once you've decided that you can and should have a substantial and successful business, and you've looked critically at where your business isn't performing, and you've discovered what you need to learn, then you need to get out there in the real world and practice, practice, practice until you are great .

The buck stops with you.

Kendall SummerHawk describes:

I got really serious about learning about marketing. I started paying, not just taking free classes; I paid for marketing courses that were organized towards coaches. And it worked. By making that investment, I stepped up. I learned how to give a teleseminar, and I started listing free teleseminars. I gave three to five free every week for about five years.

I wasted a lot of those teleseminars because I didn't know how to make an offer. It was more like hope and pray. It was a great playground for finding out what people were keen on and what they were interested in. But I also wasted some long years.

I now know how to really focus on what's going to bring in the money. I know how to get much more specific about income opportunities.

TOTAL RESPONSIBILITY FOR YOUR REACTIONS

Viktor Frank tells his story in a moving autobiography "A Man's Search for Meaning." He was an Austrian Jew, and a professor of psychoanalysis at the time of the Nazi invasion. He was put into a concentration camp, all of his possessions taken, his wife and family destroyed. The only thing he had managed to save was a manuscript, his life's work. He had sewn it into the lining of his coat. When he got to the concentration camp, the guard collected all of the clothes including the coat. Viktor asked to salvage his manuscript, the only thing left in his life that was important to him. The guard ripped open the coat and examined the papers. The guard looked at them carefully and went to hand them back to Viktor. As Viktor reached his hand out to take them, the guard snatched them back out of reach, and laughed as he tore them up and trampled on them.

At that point, Viktor had lost everything. But he made a decision, and this decision was critical. He decided that his will could not be subdued. That his optimism wouldn't flag. Over the following years, he watched his fellow prisoners give up. And as they gave up, they slowly let themselves fall behind; they soon got sick, and they stopped looking for extra food. They starved more quickly and then succumbed to illness and a rapid death. There were a few others who also did not give up. They believed that although everything physical had been taken from them, and although every-thing emotionally significant had been taken from them, life would still have meaning for them.

TOTAL RESPONSIBILITY FOR YOUR COMMITMENT

You can't control all of your external circumstances. However, you have control over your feelings about your business. You will experience setbacks in your business; they are inevitable. But it is how you respond that will ultimately set the scene for how well you bounce back from them. The most successful women look at their challenges as things that they are able to overcome with support and perseverance.

Linda Simonsen has one of the most challenging stories. Her business has considerable cash requirements, as the staff needs to be paid well in advance of when the employer pays her contract. During the GFC, this cash pressure intensified...

I remember during the GFC, orders had dried up, there was no work, and we were like a pub with no beer. But we had a large group of temps on-site working for a large client that was backed by two major banks. I was off in Thailand, and I got a phone call from my team. They were all in the boardroom, and I thought, 'How nice! They're ringing me to say happy birthday! I didn't know they liked me that much!' And, of course, they weren't. They were calling to tell me that our client had been placed in administration, and that there were 400 people congregating around our office. They wanted to know what to do, and I said, 'Well, put the barbeque on.' These people had just lost their jobs, so we made our sausage sizzle and registered them to look for work through us.

At the same time, some of those people were our temps, and, of course, the client wasn't able to pay their wages. So in the middle of the GFC, I had a healthy business, had done all the right things, and there was the real potential risk that I would lose everything I owned because one client had gotten into strife.

I learned about preferential payments and call backs, and I called an urgent meeting with my Entrepreneur's Organisation group and asked what they knew about administration receivership and how I could protect my business, my people, and my assets from a mistake that had nothing to do with us.

In the end, it was amazing. This group of people had such a wealth of experience – buying, selling businesses, failing businesses – and they reached out to their network and came up with a strategy to get my business through it. We actually ended up profitable that year while 30% of our competitors went under.

TOTAL RESPONSIBILITY FOR YOUR COMPETITIVE RESPONSE

You need to take responsibility for the direction of the business. Your business will do its best when it has a clear direction and you are clear about what you are moving toward. It will be more likely to thrive when you are clear about what your competitive advantage is, and what the secret sauce is that makes your offering unique in the marketplace.

You can't control what your competitors do, but you can predict that they will try to innovate and lower their costs, and that new people will start businesses in your field and try to build strong relationships with your clients.

How do you respond to this? Do you feel worn down by the inexorable onslaught of competition? Do you take it personally and start to feel battered by the attack? Or do you feel inspired to create more innovative products that deliver value in different ways?

All of these responses are valid, but only one will give you the energy and momentum to be able to stay in the game. It all depends on what you want.

If you want to make your business a success, then you need to recognize that there will be challenges from sources beyond your control. You need to prepare for the unexpected, so you know that when you are challenged, you can develop a creative response.

Total responsibility means that your response needs to be strong.

STAY ENGAGED AND LOOK FOR OPPORTUNITIES

When you're put into a situation where you have to find your inner strength and courage, you might decide to do nothing at all.

Sometimes doing nothing is a great tactic, particularly if you're trying to make a decision – the benefits of fast decisions can be overstated. But if business is suffering, you must be engaged in the process and understand what's going on, quickly. Opportunities to make things better in business can pass quickly, and opportunities to make giant advances in revenue can also be fleeting.

There's a beautiful story told in the Richest Man in Babylon (required reading for any female entrepreneur).

A young livestock trader locked outside the city gates one night was approached by an elderly man. The elderly man had been waiting to enter the city the next day to sell his livestock at the markets. He had been called away urgently as his wife was sick and had no time to wait for either morning or the markets. He asked the young man to buy the flock at greatly discounted prices. The young man refused, saying that he needed to see the flock and to count them in the morning. The elderly man pleaded, discounting the flock even further. The sound of the livestock was great, and the young man knew that if the size of the flock was told to be true, then he would make a considerable profit. But he refused again, insisting on the need to count them. The elderly man did the deal elsewhere, needing to be away. The next morning, the young man saw the flock was even larger than he first thought and kicked himself because the opportunity had passed him.

The same is true for your business. There are times when the need for an engaged response is critical. If you are looking to grow your business, then you have an obligation to learn how to sell properly and how to develop a highly effective follow up system. You have an obligation to price your services so that they give exquisite value to your clients while also rewarding you for your unique contribution.

If you decide to give up and go home during a difficult period, then your business will give up, too. What you do sends a message to your staff, your team, your clients, and your investors.

Your response determines your future.

KNOWING THAT YOU CONTROL YOUR RESULTS HAS ENORMOUS POWER

There is some great research supporting the idea that feeling in control gives you positive reinforcement. Early research by Julian Rotter, published in 1966, called the "Locus of Control," deals with the way we feel about decisions and our lives, whether controlled by us or by outside factors.

If you believe that the locus, or the source, of control is somewhere outside of you, and that you have no influence over what happens to you in your life, then you will start to feel quite helpless and your ability to achieve will decrease.

On the other hand, if you believe that you have control

over your circumstances, then you'll feel more motivated to achieve. You'll believe that success is up to you, and you'll be inclined to chase after it.

For example, you might receive a poor score on a test. If you have an internal locus of control, you'll believe that you were responsible for the test result, and, therefore, the blame (as well as the opportunity to improve) lies within you. If you have an external locus of control, then you'll blame others, thinking that it was probably the teacher or the test itself which was to blame.

THERE ARE ALWAYS CHOICES

If you decide that you want to continue moving forward, but you don't currently have the strength to continue yourself, you'll have to create an environment that supports your forward momentum.

Carey Peters sometimes finds it hard to keep up the momentum by herself, so she has invested in a business coach and a mind set coach and surrounded herself with people who keep her moving forward.

What I didn't understand years ago, and what I think many people don't understand, is that you are going to want to quit. You are going to be afraid, you are going to be full of doubt, and there are going to be challenges and obstacles all along the journey. I was able to keep going by investing in coaches and mentors.

In the beginning, I didn't see how I was going to keep acting [my first passion] and run a business. In 2011, my business partner Stacey and I did our first live event. I remember asking her, 'Do we really have to do this? Can't we just cancel? Can't we just put it off?' Her resounding response was, "No. This is the next step. We have to do this." It was very successful, despite being such a financial risk.

Before that event, I was tempted to quit because I really thought my main identity as an actor was being threatened. But because I could actually make a living from my business, I could pick and choose the acting projects that I wanted to do. As an actor, you don't always have that luxury. Now, I love live events - it's an extraordinary experience to get in a room with people and work for three days on professional and personal growth.

DOWN TO BUSINESS – HOW TO COMMIT TO YOUR BUSINESS

You've decided that you want to grow your business. You know why you want to grow your business, and you've created a vision for where you want to go. It's now time to commit and get into the nuts and bolts of your business strategies.

Being a leader means being able to communicate your vision. Once you can do that effectively you can start to enlist other people who will help bring your vision to life. These people can be your clients, your team, or even supportive friends.

Exercise: Take a piece of paper and answer each of the questions below. If you don't know the answer to every question right now, that's okay. Consider this an ongoing exercise as your business progresses:

1. Review your vision for where you want your business to be in five years time. Consider the results that you get for your clients, rather than the process. For example, if you help entrepreneurs with their businesses, you'll describe the business growth that they get, rather than the strategic review that is part of your process.

2. Write down who your ideal clients are. How many are there? Are you working one-on-one or in a small team or with large organizations? Do you have multiple streams of income, including passive income from home study courses or membership sites? How well-known are you? What impact do you want your business to have on the world?

3. Decide what your number targets are for this year and next year. You'll want top-line revenue and profit percentage as an absolute minimum. You might have other measures that you want to keep track of, but try not to have more than 10 measures that you look at on a monthly basis.

4. Know whether you want most of your business to come from existing clients or new clients – and

if you are going to have any substantial change of direction with either the client base you're working with or with the programs and services that you offer. This is going to have a significant impact on the type of marketing work that you do.

5.   Write down your strategies to nurture those clients and turn them into paying contracts. Service-based professionals have a huge number of marketing and visibility strategies to choose from, but without significant support, you will be better off choosing no more than 4–6 and doing them well.

6.   Share this information with clients, your team, and friends. You will probably choose to hold back the revenue numbers and the profit target. However, your clients and your team will really appreciate knowing your vision for your business and will admire you for doing the work.

Once you have mapped out your answers to each of these questions, you will have some solid business strategies in place.

IF YOU ACT AS IF YOU ARE POWERFUL, YOU WILL BE

Other research lies in understanding the whole "fake it 'til you make it" approach.

If you start to feel as though you are no longer in control, and you want to throw the towel in, then you can use some physical methods to help get you mentally back in the game. Amy Cuddy, an associate professor at Harvard University, has done some elegant research with Dana Carney at UC Berkeley (published in 2010). Together, they found that non-verbal expressions of power, such as the way that you stand, the postures that you hold, and how much space you take up in the world, have a physical impact on the hormonal response as well as how you think.

If you "fake" a body posture that is associated with power (i.e. pretend that you are powerful by holding your body a certain way), then you will find that your testosterone increases, your stress hormone, cortisol, decreases, and your appetite for risk is increased. The effect is summarized succinctly: "If you act powerfully, you will begin to think powerfully."

REACH OUT FOR SUPPORT

Do a candid assessment of your strengths and opportunities. You might have unrealistic expectations about money and how much you are capable of creating through your business. You find it challenging to stick to your plans or struggle to find the courage to follow through.

A good tool to help you review is the downloadable Assessment sheet, which is given as a bonus download with this book (see the end of each chapter). If there are gaps between where you are and where you want to be, seek help.

CHAPTER SUMMARY

* Building a seven figure business takes commitment and a level of responsibility beyond what most people will understand.

* The journey might be longer than you think when you first start out – don't give up.

* You control the level of your success. Knowing that you control your results gives you enormous power.

* Be clear where you want to take your business, know your vision, goals, and strategies. Know your growth model and your numbers.

* Communicate your vision and your message, so that you bring people with you.

BONUS DOWNLOADS

Visit the exclusive resources section of the book at
www.oneextrazero.com/catapult/bonus

Take the downloadable assessment and discover how strong is your Catapult: A Woman's 7-Figure Business Quotient.

Download a Sample Template for Simple 1 Page Business Plan

CHAPTER 4

YOU WILL BE PERSONALLY CHALLENGED

"If you think about it, any business problems are simply personal problems in disguise."
—Michael Port, Book Yourself Solid

The journey of building a business that turns over seven figures a year isn't likely to be like gently flowing into a river of riches, more often than not your journey will be like walking through fire as you rely on your spirit and character to get you through.

The challenge is to hold a vision of success steady in your head while you take on the total responsibility of pushing your creation into the world. Make no mistake you will be challenged.

You will have to learn new skills, and forge new inner strengths. You will have to meet people and share the vision of what you want to achieve. You will need to communicate in such a compelling way that people will be moved to work with you to help you achieve your goals.

Building a business is a crash course in personal development. When you have no one to rely on except yourself, you'll have to be brave enough to sit with yourself and not freak out. As challenges and obstacles confront you, your weaknesses will be amplified; they can't be avoided. "Your stuff will come up," as one interviewee succinctly put it. Your growth will be tremendous as you work through your personal obstacles and transform into a higher version of your previous self.

Such a transformation can take its toll. As the inner self changes, so will the outer. You might find that some of your relationships no longer support the person you are becoming. Perhaps when you seek guidance from friends and family during times of crisis, there is a limit to the level of support that they can offer. You need to surround yourself with people who can support your transformation and who believe in your vision of yourself and your business. During times of self-doubt, those people will hold steadfast to your vision, even when you can't.

BELIEFS

Mindset drives everything. Your mindset is what you believe is possible. The external world is a manifestation of what's happening within your mind. If you haven't come across this concept before, bear with me.

Your external world, your reality, is determined by how you see yourself in life. When you imagine what your ideal world looks like, and then open your eyes to find that you're in a different reality, it's your beliefs that have prevented you from achieving what you had envisioned.

This concept is sometimes better explained by looking backward, rather than forward: If you think back to a relationship from your past that you weren't particularly impressed with, in hindsight you can probably see that you were the one who accepted the terms of the relationship, even when it was less than satisfactory, and the one who continued to stay in that relationship.

Perhaps for you it wasn't a personal relationship, but a job that you didn't enjoy and which brought you misery and unhappiness. You had the choice to accept that job and to stay in it, even after you realized that it was causing you unhappiness.

You have an enormous amount of control over how you see the world. Have you cast yourself as a success or as a victim? Do you see yourself as fragmented and not focused enough? Do you think that those who have found success have more time than you? That they're smarter than you? That they're luckier than you?

When you realize that you have the power to control the beliefs that are holding you back, you'll discover that you can change your external world. It's an incredible realization.

You will discover that the patterns of your mindset guide your thoughts, which impacts every decision that you make and every action that you take. Because your decisions and actions are ultimately driven by your mindset, what you believe is possible will influence everything from your level of confidence to the challenges you accept.

Challenging an existing belief is a bit like having a miniature seismic attack in the brain and body. Sometimes it is intentional, but other times, it comes quite out of the blue. Sometimes I will share an opinion with a friend, and she will ask, 'Is that really true?' When I take a moment to think about it, I realize that it's not true and it's only my assumption, and another layer of possibility opens up before me.

Your belief system will allow you to either rise to the challenge or be overwhelmed by it. It's not just a matter of having a positive frame of mind; you need to hold a belief that you can become proficient at skills or situations that you haven't yet experienced. It's called a growth mindset.

MINDSETS KEEP OUR BRAINS FROM EXPLODING

Given how limiting our mindsets can be, it's not unusual to wonder why you have them at all. It's a protective mechanism. Your mindset allows you to filter out what you can't deal with. The world has so much detail in it that if your brain processed all of it all at once, you would be overwhelmed. Without that filter you would be so busy processing information about the texture of your clothes, the breeze in the leaves, and the white noise hum of the photocopier that you would never get anything done!

Our brains have created shortcuts. We look for patterns that tell us, refrigerator white noise – normal – no need to pay attention there. Clothing texture – normal – pay no attention there. Those shortcuts allow us to filter out sources of information that have no value so that we can focus on the things that are important to us.

Equally, other patterns demand our attention. Baby wakes up, we take notice and do something. Fuel light goes on in the car, again, we take notice and do something. Rampaging elephant caught in peripheral vision, hopefully, we do something.

But when something out of the usual pattern emerges without a signal linked to immediate action, we are faced with a choice to either accept or reject it. We have to take a conscious look, which is such hard work for our brain. So we try to force the information to fit into the usual pattern, just so that we can process it quickly and move on.

A business opportunity might come along with a bigger client. If your belief is that you're already busy and can't take on more work, then you won't be able to see the benefits of the situation – which might be that a bigger client might value your work at a higher level, allowing you to drop some of your smaller projects and ultimately work fewer hours.

MINDSETS HAVE PROVEN VALUABLE FOR THE SPECIES

On the other hand, your mindset can be valuable, especially when it comes to protecting you from risk. If you decided to act on every risky impulse, then there's a good chance that something very bad would happen to you. Our mindsets protect us by keeping us in our comfort zone. A few people in the population have "outlier" status when it comes to their risk tolerance for trying new things, such as exploring new continents, crossing unknown oceans, climbing mountains, that sort of thing. But it doesn't make sense for an entire population to possess this high-risk attraction. From an evolutionary point of view, it makes much more sense for a small group to take the risks and then report back to the larger group.

The good news is that your mindset is quite different from the risk profile of an explorer. We're not talking about crossing an ocean that may or may not represent the edge of the world. There is no physical danger here. There are only the mindset constraints that bind us.

So when you set off on your entrepreneurial voyage, you need to recognize that reaching out for bigger clients, or becoming more visible, or hiring new team members, is part of the journey that won't put you in physical danger. That's just the old mindset trying to keep you where you were (less risk), so you don't have to do the mental work of exposing yourself to new things.

Carey Peters found that as her business grew, she also grew significantly as a person. She talks through her transformation.

My life lesson was to choose myself, and there is not one single area of my life that has not been transformed. I overcame an eating disorder; I was $70,000 in debt, even going into building my business. I got out from under that debt, and I built a strong financial foundation for myself.

I had such turbulent relationships in the past, and now I'm in a really wonderful relationship, solid and fantastic, and I have a beautiful home; I never lived in a place so lovely. I always had kind of crappy little apartments. The other thing is that I'm still performing. I still do musicals. I traveled to California for a show, but I live in Chicago, and my business is growing on top of all of that.

On the inside I changed, too. There were so many ways in which I felt I was not worthy or worth it. In an audition room, I would never pick myself. My life lesson was to choose myself instead of somebody else. Even in my first business, people would ask me to coach them, and I would say, 'No, no. You should go over there to work with so and so.' This transformation happened over a period of four years. It's extraordinary, and I feel really blessed.

WHERE DID THESE BELIEFS COME FROM?

Most of your beliefs were established by the time you were seven years old. Still just a kid. They evolved from the beliefs of your parents and teachers and especially your peer group. These beliefs have reinforced themselves throughout your life as you have sought out and become friends with people who share your belief system.

Think of your mind as a music player that can play any type of music that you want and a belief as music track. As a little kid, you didn't have much choice about what music was playing. You had to listen to the music that your parents wanted to hear or that they thought was suitable for you.

As you grew up, you went to school and to your friends'

homes, and you started listening to music that your teachers or your friends' family likes, and then you picked up those tracks as well.

So by the time you were grown, you had a selection of music that the people around you had chosen for you. You haven't had a chance to go and sample all that the world has to offer. If it turns out that your parents only liked classical Spanish guitar, and your friends were into punk rock, then you're going to have a polarizing collection of tracks to choose between. You also don't have a way of knowing if bubble gum pop or a capella barbershops are the things that really make your heart sing.

When you do finally decide to take charge of the tracks that are going through your head, it's like going through your music library and discarding the music that you don't listen to anymore and don't need to carry around as baggage. Only then can you start to proactively choosing music that supports the emotional and physical states that you want to be in.

THE STORY OF THE ELEPHANT

When an elephant is a baby, and taken from its mother. A heavy rope is tied around its leg, with the other end securely fastened around the base of a large, sturdy tree. The baby elephant struggles (this is not a nice process) to get back to its mother. Eventually, it learns that the rope is stronger than it is. It becomes conditioned to believe that the rope securing its leg cannot be escaped.

And so, as the elephant grows, the mahout changes the rope gradually so that it is thinner and lighter, and it is secured not to a sturdy tree but to a flimsy stake in the ground. The now-grown elephant feels the rope around its leg and believes that it cannot be free. It doesn't know that it is strong and could pull the stake out of the ground with a sharp tug and walk away.

Our belief systems are like the ropes that bind the elephant. They are ingrained in us when we are too young to reject the ideas. We are trained to believe that we are stuck in a particular rut and cannot see that the rut is of our own creation.

The beliefs that bind us to our current life are not the beliefs that are going to move us to the next level. If you want to have a business that is turning over seven figures – or more – you will need to have a different set of beliefs than the ones you hold today.

YOUR BELIEF SYSTEM

You hold a set of beliefs that guide you now. I don't know what yours are, but I am certain that you have them. Most likely they come from a time when you were a child and didn't have the ability to determine if they were beliefs that you did or didn't want to hold. Not only did you not have the experience to judge them, but you also didn't have the cognitive ability to reject the ones that were not useful for you.

You can test what some of your beliefs are quite easily when you are posed with a question. Notice your responses. For example,

Women who build multi-million dollar businesses from scratch are (check all that apply):

- ☐ To be admired for their achievements
- ☐ Driven purely by money
- ☐ Connected to their purpose and their message
- ☐ Selfish and self-aggrandizing
- ☐ Likely to give large donations to charities that they support
- ☐ Trying to be like men
- ☐ Excellent role models for my own children
- ☐ One-dimensional, cold women who don't have time for friends or family

While these might seem extreme, they represent the wide range of beliefs that different people actually subscribe to. The boxes you checked represent beliefs that you hold.

If most of the beliefs that you checked were negative, it is unlikely that you will build a successful multi-million dollar business from scratch because you hold a negative association about the type of woman who does.

It's strongly recommended that you spend some time with the people who are already at the place where you want to be. Not only will it give you an opportunity to disabuse yourself of any misconceptions about what successful women are like, but you will also have an opportunity to understand their habits, their mindsets, and the way that they approach their own businesses and life.

HOW DO I KNOW IF MY BELIEFS AND MINDSET ARE THE ONES I WANT?

The best test is to close your eyes and envision your ideal day in exquisite detail. Imagine waking in the morning. Who you wake with and what room you awaken in? How do you feel after a day with your business or on the weekend spending time with your loved ones? Imagine your home, the furniture, the kitchen, the lounge, your bedroom, and bathroom. Imagine the hobbies and pastimes you have in this ideal life.

Now, open your eyes and consider what your home looks like and feels like right now. Consider what your business looks like, who you work with, and what you do. Consider the relationships close to you. How do you feel after spending a day with the people close to you?

If there's a complete match between what your ideal life is and what your current reality is – well done!

If, however, you're like the other 99.9 percent of people, then there's a gap between what your ideal future looks like and where you are today. If you have reasons or excuses why there is such a gap, then it means that your mindset doesn't believe that this imagined ideal life is possible for you.

Don't be too disheartened. You are on a journey of personal growth, which means that you will be a greater person at the end of it. You will have overcome the invisible beliefs that have held you in place. And although you might still feel like 'you' on the inside, the changes will be visible in the results.

Leela Cosgrove has transformed as her business has grown, but still feel the same on the inside.

If you talk to people who know me really well, they will tell you I'm a completely different person. But it's really hard to see that. To me, I'm still the same little seven year old girl who used to get bullied in primary school.

I created a $1 million business before age 35. I think in your head you really never change. In your head, you're just you, and it's always amusing that people see you as being big.

The biggest thing that has changed is my mindset about money. I was always tenacious and hard working, but I used to have a lot of fear about money – getting it and not having enough of it. It's understandable when you've only earned about $30,000 a year. I came from a working class background, so I did get a lot of that negative, 'Money doesn't grow on trees. Rich people are evil. If you're making money, you're screwing somebody over.' I had to do a lot of work to get rid of that kind of mindset.

I also learned that in order to double and triple your business, you have to double and triple yourself. So you go through immense personal growth spurts, and most of the people around you won't understand that. I know people who have lost family in the process. My mother and sister both work for me now, and we have had our fights, but I've been very blessed to have a family that's incredibly supportive.

Patterns can be formed early on in life, and are often not conducive to the reality that we want for ourselves. For example, the mindset of "go to college, get a good job" is rarely enough to create the life of your dreams.

The good thing is that patterns are easy to change, and the more that you immerse yourself in a new paradigm, the faster you reprogram your subconscious. When you are faced with a challenge, you might find that the old pattern will try to reemerge. You need to be strong and recognize that fear and doubt are not truth. You need to remember that you can find a new truth whenever and wherever you choose.

Shelene Taylor agrees that her transformation has been profound.

I've discovered capabilities in myself and confidence in my abilities that I didn't have before. I used to be really shy, really reticent, and very introverted. As a kid or young adult, I did not have a lot of confidence in my abilities. And, just recently, I feel like I have blossomed into who I really am. I feel like I'm really expressing myself in ways I never have before and have learned how to be really masterful and really graceful when working with other people. So, on a personal level, I feel that I am still in the process. I think it's an ongoing journey of becoming who I'm meant to be. Each of us is unique, like a snowflake or a fingerprint, and we forget that. We really do. We try to be like other people and try to make other people happy. Particularly, I think, as women. And that's what I did for my whole life until fairly recently. Now I feel perfectly beautiful and competent and okay with how I am and who I am today and what I can bring to each person that I interact with.

THE IMPORTANCE OF A GROWTH MINDSET - THERE IS A REWARD FOR WORKING HARD

The work of Stanford Professor Carol Dweck brings incredible insight into the study of mindset and its role in success. Her book, Mindset: The New Psychology of Success, comes highly recommended.

Dweck's research suggests that the brain can change itself; she calls it the "Expandable Theory of Intelligence." If you believe that you are dumb, then you will stay dumb. If you believe that you are smart, unfortunately, according to Dweck, there's not much advantage. While you will do well in the work that requires little effort from you, in the face of adversity you will crumble. You will become scared of failing and of no longer being called "smart," and so you will pull back from challenging yourself and attempting things that you are not already excellent at. And, if you never challenge yourself, you can never improve.

On the other hand, if you believe that you can teach your mind to learn new things, and you understand that your brain changes when you learn new skills, you will be open to developing new mindsets, which then allow for new neural pathways to be formed.

One of her experiments took a class of schoolkids and put them through an eight-week program. In the control group, half of the kids were taught study skills. The test group, the other half of the kids, were taught study skills AND how they could learn to be smart. This latter group learned that the brain was like a muscle that grows stronger the more it is used. In just two months, the students from the second group, compared to the control group, showed significant improvements in grades and study habits. "It was the motivation," Dweck said, "The students were energized by the idea that they could have an impact on their minds."

Ariel Hyatt decided to learn how to value herself and her time. The evidence was all around her, but until she started to examine it, her mind tried to keep her in a place of inertia.

I think that the biggest change is I'm just beginning to really understand my power. I managed to operate a social media business in the black through a global economic recession whilst the music industry crumbled around me, and I never even understood that what I had done was a big deal.

I think part of my breakthrough came from realizing that I work in an industry where the paradigm is like getting blood from the stone. Then, I realized my real value and what people outside the music industry were actually paying for the exact same work I was doing. My self-worth wasn't only tied up with how much money was going into the bank, it was also tied up with the mission that I wanted to put out into the world and what I wanted to say and how I wanted to affect artists. I was getting accolades and invitations. I had a bestselling book and a university course named after me, and I thought, 'Why am I still charging $3000 for a three month campaign? What on earth am I doing?'

I came to understand that I was literally squandering my talents and had outgrown the vast majority of my client base. That was my tipping point, and I doubled and tripled my prices almost overnight. I fired my Director of Sales, sat down with my team, and said we've got to get better at what we do because we're going to start charging three times as much. And I started saying no for the first time.

WHAT DOES THIS MEAN FOR WOMEN IN BUSINESS?

If the image of your ideal life and your current reality don't match up, then you can change your beliefs and start to take action. The world is full of enough failed dreams already. You have an obligation to yourself to live your own ideal life.

Take a proactive view about the skills that you need to improve. If you're not good at sales or marketing, then the first step is to recognize that you can become good at them with training and practice. The next step is to find somebody – or something – to learn from. This could be a book, a home study course, or a mentor who is proficient at sharing knowledge.

You can learn to be the leader in your business. You will need to know where you want to take your business as well as the skills you'll need to get there. For example: Even if you're working alone now, you'll most likely want to find other team members to help you fulfil your greater purpose in the future, in which case you will need learn to lead a team in order to take your business to the next level.

You have to believe that you can learn it, and the research tells us that you can.

You know this already. You already know that children are constantly learning new skills and improving old ones. If you've seen a toddler catch a ball and a teenager catch a ball, then you know that skills improve with time and practice.

Consider the skills you have learned as an adult. It might be managing a household, learning to drive, raising kids, or caring for relatives. Starting a business and building a business requires different skill sets, but these skills can still be learned.

You might not be proficient at every element just yet. If you believe that you can be proficient, then you will continue to grow and learn.

Natalie Archer talks about finding herself outside her comfort zone on a very regular basis. It's a necessary part of her journey and not an option.

Your learning zone is not in your comfort zone, right? When you're in your comfort zone, it's because you are doing something you are already good at. Your learning zone, by its very nature, means you're breaking new ground, so most of the time when you're out there, you'll be thinking, 'Can I really do this? Why are they looking at me like that?' These feelings come from being exposed. For me, this happens constantly, which is a good thing because it means that I'm stretching. It means that something good's going to come from it.

It could be a massive mistake that you're going to learn from, or something you didn't know about yourself that makes you realize, 'I can now do this, and I really didn't know that before.' I wrestled with it earlier in my career, so I worked hard to move outside my comfort zone. I would agree to something, but in the morning I would think, 'Why on earth did I agree to do a keynote?' I'd lose sleep, then I'd do it and be surprised by how rewarding it was.

Step outside your comfort zone, but remember that if your efforts fail, you're not a failure. You were simply trying something that you have never done before, and you will be better at it next time.

ENVIRONMENT

Your environment is the physical and emotional manifestation of your life. As you begin your inner transformation, by rising to challenges, building perseverance, having faith in yourself and creating discipline with your time, then your outer environment will also begin to transform.

Your outer environment includes the relationships with the people closest to you, including your life partner or spouse, friends and family, as well as your physical environments like your home and office.

YOUR ENVIRONMENT NEEDS TO SUPPORT YOUR TRANSFORMATION

When you're going through a period of intense growth, you will need support. This can't be understated. If you have a partner who is not supportive, then you'll find that your own needs are consistently subsumed by the demands of the household or by the needs of your partner. If you aren't able to make your own needs a priority then you won't have the physical time or the headspace to focus on the needs of your business. If you have a partner who is downright oppositional, you'll find yourself struggling to keep up the willpower and momentum to support yourself and your business.

Not only do you have to deal with your own personal

challenges while growing a business, you also have to deal with external challenges. You might have competitors who become more active in your space or need a greater range of innovation to remain competitive. Your ability to demonstrate value might be challenged, or a key customer may stop purchasing. Challenges are inevitable.

It took a huge personal challenge for Andrea Culligan to really shift to a more balanced view of managing her energy. Her environment is now more able to support the personal and business growth that she has committed to.

From 2008–2009, we were going at 100 per cent a year, but in reality I was just trying to keep up. Once that massive boom stopped, the 'Oh oh! Foundation's a bit wobbly' hit me, and everything came to a crashing halt. I got sick; I was having severe panic attacks and anxiety, and I couldn't sleep for days. I had a nervous breakdown, but I still did everything like normal and no one knew, and the business still doubled that year. Whether that was the right or wrong way to handle it, I don't know; it's just what I did.

The doctors told me it would take a year to recover; I gave them six months. I still had sporadic attacks through the next few years, and I still feel when it's coming on again. They're much more manageable now, and as a huge believer that what you put into your body, you get out, I now do yoga several times a week and seek expert help to manage my energy around people that don't really add value to my energy. Sometimes people that you thought would be amazing pillars of strength just aren't; when you turn to them, they shrink away. That's been the most confronting part of this whole process – realizing that those you felt you could count on the most, you really can't count on at all. It's not their fault; they just don't know how.

People might think that when these things happen to them that their life stops. Your life doesn't have to stop; it's how you choose to deal with it. What works or doesn't work for you is the thing that matters.

What you focus your energy on expands. So, as you build your million-dollar business, you'll need to focus your energy there, and you'll need to avoid being distracted by an unsupportive environment whether it is your relationships or physical or emotional issues. Make a commitment to spend less time on things that drain your energy or take your attention away from where you want to direct your focus.

RELATIONSHIPS

Jim Rohn, paraphrasing George Bernard Shaw, said, 'You are the average of the five people you spend the most time with.'

Relationships are the cornerstone of every life. Whether or not you talk about your business in detail with your spouse or your friends, you'll still be able to have a sense of whether they support you on your journey. If you have close relationships with people who believe in you, then you'll be energized and supported on your journey.

This is often the most controversial topic involving success. Looking at who you spend time with is the same as looking at the people you are influenced by. A lot of women are fearful of losing friends or being judged as being "superior" because of their success. It's hard to give guidance on individual friendships but a good rule of thumb is to think about what you might regret not achieving in five years time. If the list includes something that your friends might not support, then you will need to consider whether your own success, or the comfort level of your friends, is more important to you. As you progress along your path to success you will find other people who support you.

IF YOU DON'T HAVE SUPPORT AT HOME, FIND IT ELSEWHERE

Some of my clients tell me the most intimate stories about their personal lives. I've heard, 'My husband doesn't know how ambitious I am, so I need to do my business when he's out of the home. There's no way I could work on the weekend because he wants me to be there for him and the kids.' I've also heard, 'My husband is really nagging me about getting a more permanent job; he doesn't want me working on building my business.'

I've also seen clients break out of damaging relationships and blossom with their desire and willingness to work on their businesses.

The type of support you need is unconditional support. The kind of support that says, 'I know you might not be quite where you want to be, but don't give up. You're going to make it. I believe in you.'

Kendall SummerHawk advocates getting as much high quality support as possible.

"My advice is to have support. I think it's important to be

really particular about the support that you get. I think that lots of women get mediocre rubbish support from their spouses, like, 'Are you sure you want to do that? Wouldn't ... be easier? You can do anything, but don't you think you should get a job?' That's crap, and it's very difficult to be successful if that's what a woman's getting. So, getting support and being absolutely certain that that support is 100 percent behind you is the key. Truth telling support, not sugar-coated support, unquestionably 100 percent behind you support. Every woman has to have that, and if you have to pay for that support by being in programs, go get it. Get as much as you possibly can and surround yourself with it."

Have a look at where your relationships are and ask yourself honestly, "Does this person support me?"

If your response is, 'Well, he or she does mainly support my business, but actually now that I think about it, if his/her work and my work clash, then I'm always the one to have to stop and go and get the kids.' Or if you hear, 'He/she kind of supports me, but actually, every week at some time, he/she does say that it would be better if the income was more predictable, like when I had that job that I just hated.'

That is not unconditional support.

If you can relate to the above scenarios, then you need to start having some courageous conversations (not fly off the handle in the heat of the moment conversations) about your aspirations for your business. You want to make it clear how important this business is to you, and how you want it to be a raging success. You have to explain that you want and need your partner's genuine help and support to make that happen. Talk about your future together, and connect them with your vision so that you can openly discuss the practical things that will help, such as sharing the childcare duties, getting some home help, or negotiating a more even distribution of household chores. Whatever it takes to help you get what you need so that you can build your business.

Last year, I was asked by a client if it was possible for her to change her husband's mind about her business. My answer was this: "It is nearly impossible to change someone just by wishing it or yelling at them. The only way that your partner or anyone else will change is if they want to. So be clear on what you will and won't tolerate. It might be that when you are clear that you want their support they will start to give it." Clear communication is the first step.

PHYSICAL SPACE

Women who have built million dollar businesses put themselves in physical environments that they thrive in. I have been to the homes of several women in this book and seen pictures of many more. In every case, there is little extraneous clutter. Their space has been designed to support their own state of mind and nurture their success.

Women who have built million dollar businesses know about the need to focus on what is important and get rid of the rest. What we focus on expands, and as women with goals, we need to put intense focus into only a few things.

Some men advocate going thin and wide – throw a little at a lot and something will stick. I can't do that and neither can the other women in this book. Each woman talked more about getting clear on what needed to be done and doing that well. Not perfectly, but incredibly well. And each has a vision for the future of being even more laser focused in the areas she believes will hold the biggest opportunities for her business.

When we have fewer distractions in our life, energy moves more cleanly and clearly. Your ability to focus increases.

As you look around your environment, are you surrounded by items that overwhelm you?

You can simplify your environment and feel more fulfilled. It's counter-intuitive, but it has been proven across many fields. Consider your local supermarket. If a grocer takes out one-third of the products on the shelf, shoppers consistently report that the store has increased its range of items. That's because the decision hierarchy has been simplified. Shoppers have fewer choices to make, and because they can more easily see the choices, they believe that there are more items.

The more stuff you have around you, the more weighed down you will feel.

SIMPLIFY YOUR OFFICE

Focus on creating order and simplicity in your office space. Your time is valuable and you can't afford to lose minutes or hours hunting for client files, reference reports, or even paperclips.

The tasks you undertake in your office should also honor your need for simplicity. Repetitive tasks can be automated, simplified, or handed over to an assistant.

Surround yourself with physical things that bring you joy. While you might not have the budget to redo your home or office in the exact image of your ideal just yet, you can still make sure that your paint isn't peeling and your space is organised. Include photos or fabric or artworks that inspire you and make your heart sing.

EMOTIONAL ENVIRONMENT AND RESPONSIBILITIES

The last area that you should examine in your environment is your sense of obligation. Although not quite physical, obligations often take up physical time and energy that might be better used elsewhere. Review what you feel you "should" or "ought" to do.

For example, you might feel that you "should" go and see an old friend who is always going on about how she never sees you anymore. Since you feel guilty, you get in your car and drive an hour across town, all the while thinking that you don't have that much in common anymore. When you get there, you both talk for a bit, but the conversation lags a little because your lives have taken different directions. This leads you to start thinking about work because there are things you would rather be doing there instead, all the while your friend is talking about how much time your work takes up you begin to get a bit resentful.

Rather than spend time doing something that you feel you should be doing, and being made to feel guilty about your commitment in the process, you should put your energy into things that make you feel fulfilled and happy – in this case your work.

If instead, you met your friend and had a wonderful time that would be a different story. Watch out for feelings of guilt or resentment – they are a giveaway that your relationships might not be serving your best interests.

DOWN TO BUSINESS – YOU NEED TO IMPLEMENT SYSTEMS

Systems help you overcome challenges and give you time and simplicity, especially as your business becomes more complex. Your business, whether you are conscious of it or not, relies on systems to continue. To generate leads, convert them into customers, do the actual work, and get paid. The systems that you've created for your business might be very haphazard, or they might be quite organized and predictable.

When you start up, and it's just you, you're going to be doing everything from buying printer cartridges to chasing down invoices. But as you and your business grow and become increasingly sophisticated, you'll want to dramatically simplify your business strategy and operations by working on both your internal systems and your delivery systems.

Ideally, in your business, you want your systems to be predictable. You want to know that if you spend a certain amount of time or money on a marketing activity, you'll be able to get a particular return on your investment in the form of new or repeat clients. You'll also be able to deliver a program that has reliable results for your client.

This has two benefits. You'll give every client a similar customer experience and as a result your brand value will build in people's minds as they come to know what you stand for and what to expect from your service. The other benefit is simplicity; you no longer need to reinvent the wheel, which will save you time and creative effort. You can now put that creative energy to better use.

When it comes to your business, always ask yourself – Is this how it needs to be? Is there a way that I can simplify, or streamline, or discard something entirely? How can I improve my client's experience from a business point of view? Answering these questions will help you to simplify your systems and you'll save time, so that you can focus on more important things.

INTERNAL SYSTEMS

Internal systems are the backend of the business – the operational side that customers don't see. Remember, in order to spend 90–95 percent of your efforts on income-producing activities, you'll need your internal systems to flow as seamlessly, painlessly, and quickly as possible.

Internal systems might include your financial accounting system, your order/shipping/billing systems, your customer management system, or even your policies and procedures manual for bringing on new team members.

Investing in your internal systems is often front-loaded. You'll need to invest time up-front to save time later on.

Once you have your marketing system set up and documented, you can start to measure your marketing efforts faster and with greater accuracy. It's incredibly unlikely that you will be perfect when you're starting out, but adopting a growth mindset will help you to pinpoint what you need to learn to best meet the needs of your business. If you continually test and optimize your systems, you'll end up with a streamlined system that is highly effective for your business.

The same goes for your order/shipping/billing system. Ideally you want to have a system that somebody else can use when you're not there, and that you can eventually hand over to someone permanently, so that you are free to focus on building the business (or sleeping).

DELIVERY SYSTEMS

Making a system out of your service-oriented business is somewhat controversial. On one hand, developing a proprietary system can be instrumental in catapulting you from a sole operator into one of the 'big guys'. On the other hand, preserving every element as a customized solution for each new client can help you create an exclusive business profile with a high profit margin.

On closer examination, even the most customized solution does have a system at play. Each of the million-dollar plus businesses mentioned in this book has been focused in one specialized area. And if there were two different groups of clients, such as Ariel Hyatt's CyberPR which focused on musicians and entrepreneurs, then it was the result of a very specific strategy of transitioning the business to a new niche.

Training modules can also be easily put into a delivery system that may be able to be deployed rapidly and across multiple clients and locations. The business then becomes limited only by your ability to leverage your team and your technology.

One caution about the right time to try and scale the

business: I meet a lot of women who are captivated by the ability of the Internet to deliver their message to millions of eyeballs and wallets. But, unless you have the copywriting ability of Dan Kennedy, and the list building abilities of Seth Godin or Pat Flynn, give yourself some time to understand your customers and their very specific needs first. Kendall SummerHawk was notable because she broke the $1 million dollar turnover mark with a list size of less than 5,000 people. But others make it at 10,000 or even more.

I would encourage every female business owner, no matter what industry she is in, to create information products from the work she is already doing. It can be as simple as a White Paper that gives an update on the industry drivers, or it can be as complex as a Home Study course that provides certification for the purchaser. You might not need these immediately, but build up an inventory of assets like this and you'll be able to take advantage of them as you build your business.

CHAPTER SUMMARY

* Your belief system defines what is possible for you.

* If your reality doesn't match where you want to be, you need to change your beliefs and get out of your comfort zone.

* Your environment needs to support your transformation. This includes your physical environment where you live and work, your relationships, and your emotional responsibilities.

* Implement systems in the back end to automate and streamline. This will give you back time and will also generate fewer human mistakes.

* Wherever possible, implement delivery of work systems. Simplify and automate delivery of content and create additional income streams.

BONUS DOWNLOADS

Visit the exclusive resources section of the book at *www.oneextrazero.com/catapult/bonus*

Take the downloadable assessment and discover how strong is your Catapult: A Woman's 7-Figure Business Quotient.

Download the valuable Checklist for Processes That Can Be Outsourced or Automated

CHAPTER 5

FEAR AND DOUBT MUST BE OVERCOME

People play small for lots of reasons, but at the core of them all is fear. Playing small means playing safe - avoiding risk, failure, criticism, and the list goes on. But just imagine how incredibly different the world would be if everyone committed to playing big—taking on audacious goals, trying to make a meaningful difference, being all they could possibly be.
—Margie Warrell, Find Your Courage!

Fear and doubt are modern shackles that bind us. They're not truth, yet they have the ability to force our minds into a rut. Given that fear and doubt are not truth – though still crippling – there are ways that you can overcome them. Each time we go through the fire, we are forged a little stronger. Even women who are seemingly at the peak of their careers, with thriving businesses still encounter fear and doubt as they find themselves faced with the daunting challenge of tackling something that hasn't been done before.

It's important to take calculated risks to keep moving forward. So many women choose to play small when it comes to business. They don't take the risks that they need to take because they are scared of failure, and even more scared that they might succeed!

FEAR AND DOUBT

Now, I'm not talking about the fear that comes from physical danger. If there is a rampaging elephant coming straight towards you, it's a very good thing that you have a fearful response – the adrenaline will help you get out of the way!

The fear that I'm talking about is the anxiety that can put you into a state of paralysis. Often it happens without you even knowing it, and it's only after several weeks (or months or years) that you look around and notice that you've been stuck for a while.

That kind of fear and anxiety comes from the limbic system, the ancient part of our brain that's responsible for emotion and behavior. The limbic system wants to keep us immobile. It tells us that it is safer to stay stuck in the muck than to move into a place of uncertainty. It's so powerful that when activated, it has the capacity to shut off the rational part of our brain. Our limbic system puts up a giant STOP signal.

And so we get stuck.

WHAT FEARS ARE THERE?

Fear can occur in different forms. One of these fears is the fear of failing.

You might be frightened of losing all of your money if your business fails, or losing your income because of a situation that is beyond your control. You might even fear what a business failure says about you personally.

Another form is the fear of being judged.

Perhaps you believe that people will think worse of you because you don't have the credibility to be good enough to hire, or you may fear that people might think you're a fraud. Maybe you're afraid to be too self-promotional in case people will think less of you.

Another fear is the fear of losing love.

You might fear that when you become successful you will lose your friends or family. Maybe you think won't have time for them, or that they won't think you are still the same person. You fear that your friends might think that you want to be better than them and will pull away from you. Perhaps you're afraid that your family will become resentful because you spend too much time on the business.

You might even fear yourself changing, because you don't know what you might become.

These fears, and others like them, will stop you in your tracks, sometimes without you even being aware of them.

Carey Peters recognises that growth isn't always comfortable, and the more that you grow, the more you put yourself out there for public viewing.

Sometimes growth is really uncomfortable. I know clients will say, 'I'm worried that if I put myself out there, people might not like me, and they might not have good things to say about me.' And the answer to that is, 'You're right; they might not. There will be people who won't like you, and there will those who don't have anything good to say about you. But there are a small percentage of people who'll feel that way if you're good at what you do. It's going to be a small percentage, but it's going to happen because when people put themselves out there in a big way, it triggers people. It just does.

PARALYZING MINDSETS

Some mindsets paralyse us when we try to move forward. Doug Sundheim talks about them in his recent book, Smart Risks. They include doubts like:

* The timing isn't right.

* My ideas aren't good enough yet.

* I'm not sure what I'm doing.

* I don't want to make mistakes.

* I'll regret it if I fail.

When you get caught up in self-doubt, limiting actions come into play. You'll start playing it safe, and stop clarifying your vision. You'll stop making plans for action; and you might never even get started. You'll stop seeking opportunities to improve, and you'll being to stagnate.

If you don't take any action towards your goals, you won't succeed. It's as simple as that. And as long as you're holding onto those limiting mindsets, you will have poor performance results – both from a business and personal point of view.

Fear is more likely to be paralyzing in the early stages. As discussed in Chapter 4, adopting a growth mindset allows you to learn from your reactions to fear and doubt, and helps you see the best way forward.

Linda Simonsen found that fear was a profound motivator for her. It just wasn't an option for things not to work out, so a fear of failure was a constant companion.

I had a reception desk, a boardroom, 120 square metres of space, and for the first six months it was just me. I was driven by the fear of failure, and I think that's something that unites quite a lot of entrepreneurs. It's just not ok to not make it work.

What drove me for the first year or two was pure fear. I still have moments because I don't always make the right decisions, and things don't always go right. I went through a time when I was trying to make a big decision about investing in the business, and I had that feeling in the pit of my stomach. I know everybody says listen to your intuition, but I was still trying to learn what intuition was and what fear was.

Like many other women, I can be quite hard on myself, but by accepting that we're mortal and reflecting on our mistakes, we can look back and see that they aren't the end of the world. In fact, we might actually grow or innovate as we navigate them. Today, I remind myself that 'Tomorrow's a new day, and I'll feel differently, and I'll feel better.' There are elements of fear in all aspects of our lives including business, work, and our relationships.

Fear is frantic, while intuition is quietly assuring. I think if you sit and listen, deep down you know which is which. Over the years, I've talked to many people, and I've learned that you shouldn't make decisions until they sit well in the pit of your stomach. Most of the time, we already have the answers; we just need to be still and quiet to hear them.

WHY IT'S SO IMPORTANT TO OVERCOME FEAR AND DOUBT

If we don't overcome fear and doubt, it traps us, and we become unable to take action. It becomes an invisible rope around our leg, binding us to our current reality.

Women who own million-dollar businesses know that fear and doubt are unavoidable:

Leela Cosgrove, the self-proclaimed Marketing Brat, knows that it isn't possible to escape fear, but she has developed a good strategy for dealing with it when it arrives.

I think the only way to overcome fear and doubt is to acknowledge that it's there, put it to one side, and push through it. I still freak out when hiring a new employee because it's a really big commitment. It's money out of my pocket, it's a commitment to them, and I don't want to let them down.

Just because you hit the million-dollar mark, doesn't mean that all of a sudden you're some superhuman who has no fears or worries. You have to get comfortable with your doubts and fears and make friends with them. They pop up and say, 'Hi! Have you thought about ..., what about ..., have you covered all your angles?'

You have to walk through that fire because the prize is waiting. It's like running a marathon. You aren't sure you're going to finish. You have doubts, but you push through and do it, and you get the medal on the other side.

OVERCOMING FEAR

There are a couple of ways that you can overcome your fears. Not all of these will suit everyone, so have a take a look and decide which is right for you.

Before you can successfully overcome fear, you need to recognize what it is you are fearful of. Take a moment to think of a situation that you have been shying away from. It might be something that could do to fast track your business, or something you decided to incorporate into your business some time ago but, for various reasons, have not found the time or resources to implement it.

Hold that situation in your mind for this next section.

INCREASING COURAGE

The quickest way to overcome fear is to build up courage. Feel the fear, be brave, and do it anyway.

Ariel Hyatt found that she started to stop being so scared. She started being able to stand proud.

"The other way I finally got to seven figures was I stopped

allowing people to bully me, and I started standing up for myself.

If there was ever a client that was unhappy or started threatening me or going a little bit crazy, instead of just realizing that all I needed to do was talk to that person, I would immediately call the lawyer or someone to handle it for me. That was probably one of the biggest mistakes I made. I didn't confront people when they were upset. Because I was scared, I didn't want to hear them.

I find if people want to have a conversation, and if you just talk to them honestly, 90 percent of the time you can diffuse the situation quickly.

I don't have upset clients anymore."

Your level of courage may not be high at the moment. But, if you begin thinking of fear as a weight, and your courage as a muscle, you'll see that courage can be developed to handle stronger and stronger weights over time.

Let's say that you are afraid of public speaking. If your first attempt is just a week away, and you'll be giving training in the Town Hall to 3,000 people for a whole day, chances are you're setting yourself up for failure. But, if you start by giving a toast at a dinner for your extended family, you'll be less overwhelmed and more likely to success. Then, you can increase your 'muscle strength' by joining Toastmasters and giving an impromptu one-minute speech in a supportive environment. Next, you can work your way up to a 20 minute talk at a conference break-out group. It might take months or even years before you're running a day session at the Town Hall, but you can see how working through your fears in small steps can lead to big changes.

Public speaking is an easy one to demonstrate because it resonates with so many people. But it works just as well with any business situation: hiring staff, implementing new systems, going after larger clients, or even raising your prices.

Fear is just an obstacle that needs to be overcome. Start small, and, with time and training, your courage will replace your fear.

ELIMINATING FEAR

At some stage, developing courage won't be enough. Some of our most deeply held fears can't be overcome – even courage has its limits. In those cases, you will need to challenge your own beliefs about fear. You will need to transcend fear, so that you don't experience it at all. This can take a bit longer, but it is more powerful when you get your head around it.

For this approach, it's necessary to go back and understand that your fears come from your belief system, and you will need to challenge your beliefs in order to overcome them. Fear is created when there are errors in your own thinking. When you think about the things that you fear in the future, there is no physical danger, and there is no guarantee that the thing you fear will come to fruition. Whenever you experience fear, it's a signal that you need to shift your focus to that area; otherwise, it will continue to hold you back.

I'll continue to use the public speaking example since it still strikes a chord in so many of us. It's also a key marketing strategy for many women with professional service businesses. When it comes to establishing instant credibility and expert status, it is one of our most effective tools.

To understand your fear, it's necessary to look deeper at it. You need to pick apart what the fear is based on.

Why are you afraid of public speaking? It might be that you're afraid to make a mistake and feel embarrassed. That's pretty common. But perhaps there's some faulty logic there. Why would you be afraid of making a mistake? People make mistakes all the time, and it's possible to make a mistake no matter how prepared you are. This is particularly true if you're new to public speaking. So this part of the logic holds good. We might make a mistake.

But, why would you feel embarrassed if you made a mistake? You might feel that you're wasting the audience's time, or that you've taken the place of another speaker who wouldn't have made a mistake. Perhaps you think that the audience would think less of you if you made a mistake. These are belief based assumptions. People make mistakes all the time, even presidents and prime ministers (and people still vote for them). People make mistakes on talk shows, and they don't have to leave. So this part doesn't hold up so well. You don't know what people will think if you make a mistake, and you don't know if there will be negative consequences either.

So, while it's true that you might make a mistake. People may or may not think less of you if you do make a mistake. You really don't know, but let's say that one person in the audience DOES think less of you. Why is that important?

Perhaps because when someone else feels less about us, then we feel less about ourselves. But do we really? Is that how it works?

Your response is up to you. If they think less of you because you made a mistake, it probably doesn't matter. Don't take it personally. What's happening in their head doesn't have to happen in yours.

As you spend more time looking at your individual fears and breaking them down, they will start to seem smaller and less powerful. It is likely that over a period of months or years, consciously examining each of your fears will challenge them, and they will become smaller.

Laura Babeliowsky was afraid of criticism. As she developed her own leadership, she was able to step up and take back control of her reactions in other areas.

It's all about boundaries and vision. I was always insecure, asking myself, 'Can I really do this? I don't believe it.' I realized that something had to change in my personality. I was much too vulnerable to criticism, and that really blocked my development. I wanted to be more like women who are leaders, and I was not afraid of losing myself. And even though I knew I would change, I would also stay myself.

I had such difficulty with my assistants; I struggled when firing them, but I learned to be a leader and to always say 'I'm the person making the decision here,' even when confronting people and dealing with difficult clients.

Also, don't try to hide your vulnerability; that was an important lesson for me. Just be who you are with all your feelings and vulnerabilities. I was always thinking, 'Oh, people didn't like me, or they think I'm stupid.' Then I realized that my income was 10 times higher than theirs, which helped make me feel confident. I think money is very important, especially

*for women. Now, when I get criticized or someone doubts me,
I just think, 'Who's earning more here, you or me?'*

REACHING OUT FOR SUPPORT

Almost all of the million dollar female business owners
interviewed for this book acknowledged that fear and doubt
are par for the course. Everyone experiences it; the challenge is remembering to reach out for support.

*Andrea Culligan has built a support network she calls
her War Chest, a special battalion of armory who provides shields and protection against the fears and doubts.*

*Fear and doubt sucks, and people who tell you that they don't
fear anything are lying to you. Everyone's afraid at certain
times. My highest recommendation is to find a 'go to' person
who's not in a place of fear. When I look at my War Chest – a
group of the most incredible people I've ever met in my entire
life – they're the people that tell me 'it's all ok'. They help me
go into battle in every way, shape, or form, whenever I need
it. And they each bring a different piece of artillery: criticism,
strategy, and analysis. One even comes to kick my ass into gear.
They're the people who wipe my eyes in the back of a taxicab
and give me direction when I can't see the forest for the trees.*

*If you're living in fear and doubt, you only see one way out – by
clawing and scratching. When you remove the fear and doubt,
a plethora of options become available, and it's really important to have someone to guide you. There is always, always, a
way out. So when it gets really hard, when the fear and doubt
give you tunnel vision, you've got other people to help you say,*

'No. It's okay. This is how we can start to look at it.

There aren't any formalities with my War Chest, they're just a call away. Anytime, anyhow, anywhere, and they've all been there for me whenever I've needed them. It's the most humbling experience I've ever felt in my life. Ever!

OVERCOMING DOUBT

The other side of fear is doubt. If fear is the avoidance of risk that might lead to danger, doubt is the paralysis of indecision. It sits right in between belief and disbelief that something is true, or that an action will bring about a particular result.

Doubt appears in force when you are trying to shift your mindset. For example, you adopt a particular mindset that believe will be valuable to growing your business. Let's say you decide to believe that it's possible that "I create the exact level of my financial success." And you use that mindset to override your previous belief that, "No matter how hard I work, I just can't seem to get ahead."

When everything is going your way, it is easy to adopt this new belief (and others). The positive evidence around you reinforces this new mindset. But at the first sign of difficulty or adverse circumstances, then you'll begin to wonder if you really are capable of creating your new reality.

When you find yourself wondering, "What if...," or "But maybe...," that is doubt. You'll find it much harder to progress when you are plagued by doubt. Making decisions becomes more difficult when your mindset is clouded.

Just as fear can be overcome by using certain strategies, so can doubt. A good technique is to ask yourself what you would like to believe, and then use that to take action to help you get to your destination. Another good question to get you moving in the right direction is to ask yourself, "What do I need to do in order to excel at this?"

THE IMPORTANCE OF TAKING CALCULATED RISKS

Risks are curious.

On one hand, you'll know that if you don't take any risks at all, then you'll stay in your comfort zone, and you won't make any significant progress. You certainly won't build a million dollar business.

On the other hand, when you do take risks, you open yourself up to the possibility of failure. You step out of your comfort zone, which can make you uncomfortable, and because it's a risk, there's no guarantee that your effort and discomfort is going to bring you any rewards.

Surveys of retirees almost invariably find that the highest occurring regret is that they didn't take more risks. That they didn't leave their job, chase after the love of their life, or do something that they were passionate about. Ask yourself what you would regret not doing in five years time. The answers might be enlightening.

Kendall SummerHawk adopted a mindset "I am a million-dollar business owner" well before she was one. The results were breath-taking.

Between 2006–2007, I had another rock bottom moment. I was making money, had a very typical coaching practice (15 clients paying me monthly), did a couple of groups, and had sold a couple of home study courses. I had bits and pieces of all the right things, but my income was still very episodic. I would have a $3,000 month, then a $15,000 month. Those are pretty wild swings, and it was making me crazy.

I remember looking at my money tracking sheet (just like the one I now teach), and saying, 'Wait a second! This is ridiculous! This is not going anywhere'. That's when I came to rock bottom and decided to take a risk. I made a decision to up my game in terms of a group program, and I designed a pretty innovative one. People signed up, and it kicked off with a live event – a 50 person live event! At that live event, I up-sold for the first time, and I hit six figures literally overnight.

Making that kind of money overnight puts a girl on a little bit of a high, but I wondered if I could do it again. Six months later, I did! Between these groups, the low-end original group, and the high-income program, I was like somebody spinning plates. I actually broke $1 million turnover with a list of less than 5,000 people.

FRAMING THE RISK HELPS THE CALCULATION

Your brain is designed to help you avoid losses. If you focus only on what you might lose if you take the risk, then you tend not to take it. Conversely, if you focus mainly on what you would lose if you DON'T take the risk, then you are much more likely to take that leap.

There was an interesting experiment carried out in 1981,

where Amos Tversky and Daniel Kahneman looked at the ways that framing the outcome of a particular hypothetical scenario influenced how people chose to behave.

In the hypothetical example, there had been an outbreak of a particularly deadly flu virus, which had affected 600 people in total. There were two different scenarios for treatment – one that emphasized how many people might die, and one focusing on how many people might be saved. Participants were put into either Group 1 or Group 2 and only saw one of the treatment options. They were then asked to choose whether or not they would give the treatment. Here are the options:

	Group 1	Group 2
Positive frame	A. Saves 200 lives	C. 400 people will die
Negative frame	B. There is a 1/3 chance of saving all 600 people, and a 2/3 possibility of saving no one.	D. There is a 1/3 probability that no one will die, and a 2/3 probability that all 600 will die.

These four outcomes are essentially the same – that 400 of the 600 affected people will die and 200 will be saved. When the researchers looked at what Group 1 did, Treatment A was chosen by 72% of participants. However, for Group2, the Treatment C option dropped to only 22%.

What this indicates is that as long as we are focusing on what we might lose if we take the risk, we are likely to avoid it. However, when we focus on the risks of NOT taking the risk, then we are more motivated to take the plunge.

In reality we can't only look at one side of the risk in isolation. If we look only at the risk of loss if we take the action, then we are likely to never take action but if we look only at the risk of loss if we don't act, then we become gung-ho and start taking risks that are downright foolish.

The best way to calculate risk is of course to critically weigh up both sides. But remember, every decision will carry some element of risk. We can't foresee every possible event that will or won't happen, and sometimes you will just have to take a leap of faith.

DOWN TO BUSINESS – OVER-COMING FEAR AND DOUBT WHEN MARKETING

Becoming more visible as your business grows brings up fear and doubt for many women. For years, we've been taught to stay small and thus increase our likeability. The idea of not being liked can be terrifying. But your tribe is out there, and the more of yourself that you are, and the more visible you are, the quicker you will find them.

If you want your business to expand, then you will need to make it a priority to understand and overcome your fears and doubts so that you are able to keep moving forward on your journey.

Marketing is about being visible. Ideally you want to be known as very good at solving a particular problem or set of problems for a particular group of people. The more people are able to see the value in your services, the more highly they will pay you for them.

THE VALUE OF BEING VISIBLE

Imagine you are walking across an evening pool party filled with 2,000 people, and it's your job to find a new best friend. You don't know who that person is, but you know there's probably someone here who is just perfect for you. Someone who appreciates your values and loves what you've got to offer. Someone who loves how you help him or her when needed and who in turn, loves to help you.

But it's night, and there's poor lighting. Some people are drinking, some are in the pool, others are dancing, and there's always a couple making out down the hallway. These people are distracted! They are just getting on with having a good time, and they don't know about your quest to find your new best friend. Your new best friend might be looking for you, but there are so many other cool things to be doing. There are bright, shiny objects everywhere.

If you are walking through, looking everywhere for the new best friend, you're going to be able to talk to some people but not all 2,000, especially not the ones in the pool or those doing the funky chicken on the dance floor.

You are going to struggle!

But let's say, instead, that you're giving the speech at this same party – because it's actually your college roommate's party, and it's her 40th birthday. It's early enough in the night and all 2,000 people assemble on the lawn outside. You give the speech; it's about her, but it's witty, heart-warming and shows what a great friend you are.

After the speech is over, people are going to come up to you. Not everyone, but the ones for whom your speech resonated. Now instead of searching through the dark looking for the right person, the ones who might become your new best friend have found you! You'll still need to put in some work to get yourself over the line with the right person, but the hard part is done, and it's going to be worth it.

You need to be visible, and you can't let fear and doubt stop you.

What this story illustrates is that if you don't engage in marketing, and you don't get your message out there, then you'll have a gift but no one to give it to. If you don't put yourself out there you won't be able to find the people who are the best fit for you and what you can offer to the world.

Marketing is rarely advertising. In many cases, particularly for women in service industries, advertising can be ineffective and will require a whole lot of money while offering very little return.

Whether you're bootstrapping, or further along in your journey, marketing is key for women who want to catapult their businesses.

MARKETING FOR WOMEN IN SERVICE INDUSTRIES

At certain points in your business growth, you will plateau. The plateau often causes fear and doubt to rise up again, and you will need work hard to banish them.

By now, you have a good understanding of why you're doing what you do, you're clear on what your growth objectives are, who you're actually going to be serving and working with, and you have the right support systems to facilitate your growth.

Now, the challenge is to let even more of the right people know what you do. You've got to be visible and establish yourself as a credible leader in your industry.

When you first got started on your business journey, you most likely found that finding new clients was tough. Like me, you probably wasted a great deal of time connecting with people who weren't your ideal clients in the hope that you could convince them of your value.

But what's valuable is your time, and you need to focus on return on time invested. You're already busy delivering the work and most likely at least some of the back end organizing. You've got a household to manage and maybe you've even got kids to organise as well. All of that takes headspace and time. You don't want to be spending a second of your precious time on activities that don't give you a return on that investment.

We are NOT at home for Mr. Time Wastage.

For a personal professional service such as training, consulting, or coaching, unless you are running big group programs, you might want around 15–30 clients or projects. (You'll want to put your own targets here). If you're working with individuals or private clients, 15-20 clients can give you a decent six-figure income. If you are working more in the corporate market, 15-20 corporate projects can give you a decent seven-figure income.

Each of those clients will make the decision to hire you based on what they know about you and your reputation, and whether they like you and trust you. These are pretty personal factors, so you want to be building personal relationships.

You're going to be in business for a while right? While the people you work with now represent today's business, they may also come back for repeat business, and they may refer you to other people.

The strategies are (in order of effectiveness in building those personal relationships):

*   Talking to people on the phone and mastering the art of the invited follow-up.

*   Networking and referrals.

*   Speaking in person, followed by YouTube, podcasts, webinars, and teleseminars.

*   Writing articles, blog posts, newsletters, or being written about.

*   Events.

Not all strategies will suit all professions.

A psychologist won't want to make solicitations via the phone (referrals are more appropriate). And if you have a pathological fear of speaking, then networking and writing will probably suit you better.

ONE-ON-ONE CONTACT AND FOLLOWING UP

This is where you are actually spending time with your prospects, talking with them to understand what their needs are, and explaining how you would be able to assist them. There are a number of ways you can connect, from cold calling to inviting a warm prospect to lunch.

Cold calling – If your niche is changing, or if you're levelling up, there are a few different ways to get a list of new ideal clients. This works best if you can explain what you do simply, or if it is the type of problem that a prospective client would feel comfortable talking about on the phone with a stranger. You might buy a list from a commercial organization, or an assistant might build a list from LinkedIn. I know a woman with a very successful retail training business who used a telemarketing service to generate leads and build her business.

Warm calling – If you're a woman with a professional consulting business or executive coaching business, then personal relationships are going to be key. As your network moves around from organization to organization, or changes cities, then you'll find your indirect reach grows organically.

Email and letters – You can use email and letters as ways of reaching out and establishing your credentials briefly before making phone or face-to-face contact. While you may prefer to connect via email, it's unlikely that you can use this strategy in isolation to land large contracts or sophisticated buyers.

Following up – The follow up is even more important than the initial contact. As Alan Weiss points out, in business, "Absence does not make the heart grow fonder; it makes people forget." There are only going to be a small number of people who are interested in buying from you straight away. People often have other things going on in their lives. But if you are able to stay top of mind, or you come back and reconnect with them at the right time, then your ability to get new business will skyrocket. Find a system that works for you (whether a sophisticated contact management system or index cards in a old-fashioned tickler system), and use it. Personally, I teach my clients how to get people to invite them to follow up, so they'll feel welcome when they next reach out.

NETWORKING AND REFERRALS

The idea of networking often makes women feel a sinking sense of dread in the pit of their stomach. But, we can reframe it so it's not so terrifying. Let's say, "You'll go out and catch-up with some old friends. You'll also meet some new ones. Some of these will be genuine and authentic connections. You'll learn more about these people and their problems, and that will allow you to offer to solve their problems."

Networking is about building relationships with people that you are interested in staying in contact with. A great way to do this is to figure out where your ideal clients are congregating, and then go there. Don't go to places where your peers are; go where your prospective clients are.

The best introduction to a new client comes from an existing one. The introduction is warm, the need for your service is probably established, and you've come with a warm glow of recommendation. Make it easy for your clients, and give them something back in return. At least a hand-written card, maybe a special bonus extra service, and possibly a discount. Ask for a referral at least three times a year from your clients, and help them out by including some text that can be copy and pasted that gives a great overview of who you are and the results that you get.

The second best introduction is from a trusted adviser such as an accountant, lawyer, or any non-competing professional. Help these people out by making it clear who your ideal client is. Where appropriate, try to send referrals their way as well.

SPEAKING IN PERSON

Speaking in public is an enormous source of fear for so many women business owners. Practice at every opportunity, no matter how small, to build up your confidence and experience in this skillset.

Some women in business already know about the power of speaking. It's a great way to establish credibility and expertise. Speaking allows you to share an opinion, so that you can position yourself as someone who stands for something. The audience gets to see you and experience how you move and talk and interact with them.

But you don't have to speak 'in person' to be effective at getting your message out to a new audience. You might also choose to speak to your audience via teleseminars, webinars, or even YouTube – an especially great way of reaching audiences who aren't in your time zone. And, if you partner up with someone else, teleseminars and webinars will help you to reach audiences who don't yet know about you.

If you've tried doing some speaking, and failed to convert that into paying business, then you might be missing out on a couple of key strategies that will help you to connect on a deeper level with your audience and help you communicate your value. There are different ways of making an emotional connection with your audience during the presentation, and then converting those either into paying clients or at least adding them to your list.

WRITING

Writing gives you the opportunity to connect with people and build a reputation from a distance. You might write for a professional journal that reaches your ideal clients, or perhaps you've built up a good-sized list that you stay connected with through a regular newsletter. The important thing is that while giving valuable information, you also let some of your personality shine through. You want to let people know that they are hearing your voice, not just faceless corporate speak. As much as possible, you want to include a call to action that helps you build sales.

EVENTS

You don't have to have an enormous following to put on an event. One of the million dollar business owners, Leela Cosgrove, had 25 people on her list when she and her husband, Gulliver, ran their first event. They got on the phone and invited people personally, and 15 people showed up. Another owner, Kendall SummerHawk, had been at the $100,000 mark for a few years with a traditional coaching model and decided to run an event. That year, she made $564,000.

But it's not without its risks. Laura Babeliowsky ran her first event with 40 people in the audience, and not one of those signed up for her offer.

You do need to be clear that you will be able to generate business from the event. It is expensive to hire the venue, stage the event, and cater. Preparation takes time and focus, which means that there is an opportunity cost on your current business building opportunities and delivery of work.

CHAPTER SUMMARY

* Fear and doubt can be paralyzing, but there are ways of defeating or at least side-stepping them. Increasing courage, decreasing fear, or reaching out for support are the best ways.

* Don't expect fear and doubt to vanish, but do know that your ability to overcome them will continue to increase.

* Take calculated risks; look at what you will lose if you do AND don't take action.

* Continue to be build momentum and drive ever-increasing visibility until your marketing moves from push to pull.

BONUS DOWNLOADS

Visit the exclusive resources section of the book at
www.oneextrazero.com/catapult/bonus

Take the downloadable assessment and discover how strong is your Catapult: A Woman's 7-Figure Business Quotient.

Download a short audio, "Oath of Courage."

CHAPTER 6

MONEY KEEPS MOVING

Money is a result, wealth is a result, health is a result, illness is a result, your weight is a result. We live in a world of cause and effect.
—T. Harv Eker

MONEY IS ENERGY

Money is energy. Energy has velocity and movement in all its forms and struggles to be still. Sound energy and light energy travel at different speeds, but they still travel. Money has a propensity to travel, and like other forms of energy, it will generally travel to the path of least resistance.

Are you creating your business to be a path of least resistance? Given that you are the designer and creator of your business, are you reaching out to clients who are in a position to value the services you offer? Who can pay you well for what your business does? Or are you limiting your income by investing your time in developing your clientele amongst organizations and clients who believe in your skill but lack the resources to provide adequate, let alone fabulous, compensation for your time?

Are you designing your services so that they solve the most pressing problems of your ideal clients? Or are your services tinkering around the edges? Are you pricing yourself so that your clients take your services seriously? Do they have a great energetic commitment because the amount of money causes them to take the work seriously?

Carey Peters reflects on the importance of money as she built her $2 million dollar business, Holistic MBA.

Walking through the fire, for me, is actually the most important thing. The dollar figure is simply a reflection of my willingness to do that. Having a $2 million business is a reflection of who I had to become. I'm a version of myself that I always wanted to be but didn't believe I could be, and I had to walk through the fire to get there. It will probably be the same if we grow to $6 million. If we grow to $10 million, it will require the same kind of growth on my part, and so the number for me is almost like a quantitative reflection of that qualitative change.

MONEY ISN'T TIED TO ANYTHING REAL, BUT IT HAS A REAL IMPACT

As a little kid, I remember taking a $10 note to the bank to deposit into my account and being absolutely shocked that if I withdrew $10, it wouldn't be the same note. You see, I thought people put money into the bank because it was safe, and that we all had little boxes where money would sit and wait for us to need it.

I didn't realize that money keeps moving. The more money moves, or the faster it moves through the economy from person to person or business to business, then the more money there is at any given time.

Let's say that I now hold a $10 note again today. I could decide to put it under my mattress for a couple of days. That $10 note has only had an impact of $10 on the economy. It represents $10 of income and $10 of capital.

Let's say that instead of putting my money under the mattress, I donate $10 to the local kayaking sports club. The next day, the club puts some of the money in the bank and uses some to pay for repairs on the kayaks. The kayak repair guy, Chris, takes cash, so my $10 is now Chris' income. Chris stops at the local milkbar on the way home and picks up a few things, and my $10 is now with Connie at the milkbar. Connie gives her teenage son some pocket money for the local fair, and Theo takes my $10 off to the fair with his friends, and they buy some tickets for the rides. The ride manager's shift ends, and her boss gives her some cash. Now my $10 is with her. And so on. There is still only $10 in capital, but that same note represents $60 income in the space of only a few hours.

The faster it moves, the more money there is in the economy.

WHY IS MONEY IMPORTANT?

Money is a concrete and abstract concept at the same time. You can hold it, see it, and even smell it if you're holding it. But increasingly, people recognize it as just a fiat concept – numbers in a bank account on the screen of your computer. The paper (or plastic) that your money is printed on certainly doesn't match its value. If you receive money from purchases made on a computer using a credit card, and the numbers in your account go up – no money is physically transacted! Astonishing.

But this abstract concept has a very real impact on the way that you live. It impacts where you can live, what you can do in your spare time, where you eat, and how many personal staff you have.

It also impacts what you can't do – especially if you don't have it. In Australia, roughly 51 percent of female business owners do not draw an income from their business. Wherever you are in the developed world, the numbers are similar. Women generally don't have good retirement accounts. Because they have children, work part-time, and sometimes end up divorced, women find that they aren't in as good a financial situation as they'd like to be by the time they retire.

MONEY IS IMPORTANT

One of the reasons I got into my business was because I realized that building even a six-figure business still didn't give women the flexibility and freedom that they wanted. Women were leaving the corporate environment in droves to set up their own businesses and soon found that they were victims of their own success, or that they spent too much time waiting for business to come to them. But a six-figure income didn't help to build today's lifestyle and tomorrow's retirement plan in the way they had hoped. I get the greatest satisfaction from helping my clients go from six figures to multiple six figures and beyond.

Money is not the only thing in the world that is important. Love, compassion, gratitude, and an appreciation of beauty are also important. Your sense of connection and belonging and contribution to the world also matter.

But the people who have money know that money is important. Money has a definite and distinct place in the world. In this world, this modern, sophisticated, urban world, money is as important, (but in a different way and for different reasons) as love. Money can feed and clothe you. It can build roads, schools, hospitals, and even support a Social Security system.

There is no nobility in poverty. It is difficult to achieve any level of social service when you operate from a shoestring budget. Many of the best known advocates of charitable works, such as Mother Teresa, have attracted millions of dollars to advance their causes. And there are many more charitable causes that have closed shop as they failed to hit their income targets.

I cannot criticize my parents for hoping that I would never experience poverty. They had been poor themselves. And I have since been poor, and I quite agree with them that it is not an ennobling experience. Poverty entails fear and stress and sometimes depression. It means a thousand petty humiliations and hardships. Climbing out of poverty through your own efforts – that is something on which to pride yourself. But poverty itself is romanticized only by fools.

—J.K. Rowling during her keynote address
to Harvard University Commencement
Speech 4 June 2008

YOUR INCOME IS LIMITED ONLY BY YOU

If marrying into money or having a large inheritance due is not on the immediate horizon, then having a business that generates excess income is the absolutely and number one hands down best way for women to create wealth for themselves and their families.

The income that your business generates is limited only by you.

Did you get that? Your income is limited only by you. The products and services that you offer are decided by you. Your skills are malleable and can be added to. You can improve whatever you focus on and put effort into. If your income is not where you want it to be, then it is worth examining the cause of the gap.

Your skill in designing your service portfolio of offerings is limited only by you. Your customer base is decided only by you. Your skill in marketing and closing sales is limited only by you.

Ariel Hyatt stumbled into an awareness about money after a serendipitous encounter with T. Harv Eker's book, The Secrets of the Millionaire Mind, and then embarked on a personal money growth journey.

I started really looking at my business, and I realized that I was very much trapped in a paradigm. I got very comfortable, and I noticed some alarming patterns. And the first pattern I noticed was I could work really, really hard, or I could not, and I was still grossing almost the same amount of money.

That's when I realized the money stuckness that I was experiencing. It wasn't only because that's where my money dial was stuck; it was actually that I had no idea how to run a business. I was doing everything intuitively. I love music. I could go out to the band and talk to them backstage. I could sell them, but I didn't know how to run a P&L sheet. I didn't know how to project a profit.

I began to learn, "Oh, the reason why I'm not making a lot of money is because that was never even a goal. That was not even part of what I thought I was wanting to do." So the minute I made that a goal, and the minute I realized there were systems and things you could put into place to get that goal, I moved myself out of the way. Immediately, I went from $100,000 a year to $300,000 a year, literally within a few months. I had a pretty big quantum leap. And then I went up to $400,000 the next year. And then, I went up to $500,000, and I got stuck there for a while. To get to the million mark, I did two things.

The first thing that I did was hire a CFO. I didn't even understand how much money it cost to provide my services. I just *instinctively chose a number that I thought that people would be comfortable with, that felt good to me, and that was a number that I chose to price my services on. Then my new CFO, Ann, taught me all about profit margins. She said, "The good news is that you've got a half-million dollar business. The bad news is you have no idea how to price what you do. Really good businesses have a 30 percent profit margin, and you have about 5 or 6 percent. That's why you're not making a lot of money, and that's why you'll never make a lot of money."*

It was a really sharp wakeup call! It was unbelievable because then, of course, comes the mental work – the "Oh my god! I have these clients, and they're not going to pay, and I couldn't possibly raise my rate." But just by looking at the spreadsheet, I realized I was literally giving away what I did, and I shouldn't.

The second thing I did was go to the beach for seven days. I came back and tripled my prices.

WHY IS YOUR INCOME LIMITED?

It comes back to the mindset. Most women in business know that the business grows when they sell. And that they find it easier to sell their services when they are better known and have built a reputation and network of people who know and like what they do. There are systems for getting out there and generating clients, filling up the pipeline, staying in contact, and closing sales.

If you're not making as much money as you'd like to be, ask yourself if you are selling as much as you could or should be. There are, of course, other questions such as, "Are your margins in the right place?" or "Are you effectively leveraging your time to get to the important strategy and marketing work?" But start by asking if you are selling as much as you'd like.

During the interviews for this book, I asked each of the women who had built a seven figure business from scratch the following question: "If you could go back to when your business first started, what would you say to your younger self to save yourself some of the heartache?" Almost all of them said, "I would have learned how to sell earlier." Their advice: "Learn to get comfortable with selling and just do it. The risk is less than you imagine."

PAY ATTENTION TO THE MONEY AND WHERE IT COMES FROM

Money likes being paid attention to. Good positive playful energy. Only one of the women interviewed for this book started her business with an incredibly large turnover target for her business. Everyone else started it with a big vision, or as a way of finding their flexibility and freedom away from more traditional employment.

But over time, as each of these women got more familiar with the business, there was a moment when they each said, "This can be something; I can make it bigger." And an awareness of money and the management of money started being more important. Sometimes it came from inside themselves, an awareness that the business is for spreading their service wider, as well as generating a healthy reward for that service. Other times, it is brought to the entrepreneur's awareness by a trusted adviser making an intervention! The business owner is sat down and talked through the financials.

At the end of the day, money comes into your business because you have made a sale to another person or organization. You need to become good at making yourself visible, so the right people can find you, and you need to become very good at asking for the sale.

Kendall SummerHawk is a master of helping women transform their relationship with money. She reflected on her approach to marketing, time, and money.

I teach people how to be great at marketing and money. If somebody is not a marketer because their craft is something else, they still have to become excellent at marketing or hire people who are. I personally believe that anyone who completely abdicates marketing in his or her business is making a mistake. I really do. Even if he or she doesn't have the skill set to do the copywriting or to put together a campaign, that's fine, but he or she needs to understand it so that he or she can hire people and not get ripped off.

DOWN TO BUSINESS – GET GOOD AT SELLING!

SELLING AS SERVICE

It's just a conversation that helps the buyers get something that they need. And unless you are overflowing with clients with a waiting list six months long, you need to be putting yourself out there and having conversations. And if you are overflowing with clients with a waiting list six months long, then you need to be talking to someone about how to stop being a bottleneck in your own business and how to hire the right team to help you.

On top of actually doing the work, these conversations are my favorite part of business. I love these conversations because I learn so much about people. I learn what is driving them, what they want for their businesses, and what is stopping them from getting there. And I also learn why it is so important to them to be able to get the results that they're looking for.

All of this needs to come out of a conversation. You need to establish the value of working together. You need to hold a space of curiosity. You need to be willing to call them if you see something that is not congruent (i.e. it's important for them to change, but then they don't change).

You need to figure out how to make the conversation just that. A conversation. A conversation where the outcome is really clear – they need to be able to make a decision whether they want to work with you or not. If that decision isn't made, then, I'm really sorry to say it, and I'll say it as gently as I can, but you're wasting their time and yours. Now, don't get me wrong, it might take some time before you're actually hired, and you get the contract signed, and the money is with you and the work is done. But you need to leave this conversation with a committed decision as to whether or not they think there is a good fit.

SELLING MISTAKES

Here are some of the mistakes that I hear people make.

Quite often, you'll have the first conversation with a potential client, and they will ask you what you charge, and you'll tell them. They'll get a funny look, and then you won't hear from them. And they hadn't even told you what work they needed done.

Or you learn that you need to get a scope of work from your clients first – to find out what they are actually looking for. Then, you make sure you've got it all, and you give them a sense of how much it's going to cost. They ask for the proposal in writing, and you never hear from them.

Let me tell you what the gap is. They haven't been able to see the value. They have made the decision on price alone

And that's because they don't always know what that value is. People really don't like to look at their problems very deeply. So, when you outline what it is you charge, with or without a scope of work, then because they haven't discovered what the real value of getting this work done is, then chances are that you will look expensive. And they start to think about how this work can get done later.

DON'T MAKE DECISIONS FOR YOUR CLIENT

Quite often, back when I very first started out, I would decide that my potential client wouldn't want to hire me. Maybe they wouldn't need my services, or they wouldn't be able to afford me. Or, now when I look back at it, my favorite negative thought was – they should probably hire someone better. Have you ever sat across the table from someone who you think should hire someone more qualified or more experienced? It hurts, right? You have all this self-doubt, and you figuratively start punching yourself in the face – "You don't belong here; you don't have enough experience to solve this problem. Why don't you just go and get a job?"

My mindset now is, If I think that I can help this person, based on what he or she is telling me about the problem, then I can't leave until I offer my services from a place of genuine service.

It means that I don't get to decide for other people what help they need. It means that I don't get to decide for other people whether they can afford me. And I certainly don't get to decide for other people whether or not they want to work with me.

On the upside, it means that I am absolutely curious about what my potential client is trying to do with his or her business. It means that I'm absolutely clear on the value that I provide – I've seen the results that my clients get, and they give great testimonials. And if I believe that I can help them get to the place that they want to be, then it's my privilege to be able to offer that to them.

But, it means that I have to make my offer.

Leela notes that there was one thing that she should have done earlier in her business.

Sales. I should have learned sales. I spent four years in my business before learning how to sell. I went for coffee with a lot of people hoping, maybe, that one day they would give me business. I went to networking events, handed out my card, and wrote proposals for jobs that never came through because I was petrified of selling, and I didn't want to sell.

I'd been living, mind you, for four or five years with Gulliver, who managed a sales team. He had gone from being a commission-only salesperson, to being promoted to manager of the team, so he'd been telling me for years, "You need to know how to sell." I told him I didn't need to learn how to sell; I knew how to do marketing. I knew that the sales thing was something that I probably should be doing, but I was so petrified of it, and then I had that experience at the Tony Robbins' event – being on the sales table. I said, 'yeah, I reckon this could be fun. I reckon I could enjoy this. Let's do this.'

PRICING

There are so many ways to figure out how to set prices. Some recommend cost price plus a profit margin. Others look at competitor benchmarking. Still others want to add on their time or the cost of client acquisition.

These approaches are sort of okay, but they miss the point. The people who are buying your product or service don't care about your costs. In my experience, people pay for only one thing – your ability to help them understand the value of fixing their problem.

Your client has to understand his or her problem and the value of fixing it. Not everyone knows how big a problem that he or she has. People don't like to look at their problems in such detail, so you need to be courageous and have that conversation from a place of trust and genuine service.

You need to create a perception of value that is greater than the price you are charging. You also need to remember that you are in business to make money. Even if you are a consultant to the not-for-profit sector, you need to be responsible for your own financial health. You need to generate an income, so that you can keep doing good in the world. The bigger your business, the more people that you are able to bring your goodness to. This means that you need to get your head around charging for what you do.

You also need to decide which price tier you play in. A low price tier means that you need to have a higher volume of transactions to make the same money as a few transactions in the higher price tier. Quite often, women don't have the self-confidence to put themselves in the higher price tier, which means they work longer hours for the same money. They are more likely to burn out.

HOW DO YOU CREATE VALUE IN YOUR CUSTOMER'S MIND?

Bring your clients' problems to life by helping them uncover it in a story. You need to provide a solution that makes your price seem really reasonable. Focus on what the end benefit really means to your clients.

The phrase, improve the bottom line, is especially true now.

If you work with corporate, or with high functioning not-for-profits, then you want to know what measure the economic buyer needs to improve. It's either going to be revenue-raising, cost-cutting, or something that will help drive one of these two. For example, anti-bullying training is cost-cutting; as the insurance premiums rise less, retention of staff is greater, and thus spending on new hires goes down.

Increasing sales effectiveness and leadership is revenue-raising as helping your client's sales staff perform better should bring in a better return. They will feel greater engagement, be more in control of their time and their conversations, and be equipped to close the sale at a greater frequency.

How can you paint a picture that raises the stakes of the game? You need to focus on the results and the impact of the results for your client. If you are an executive coach, you need to shift the context from what it costs you each hour to have you speak to an executive, to what goals it will help your client overcome and how that impacts the organization.

If you work more one-on-one with clients, are you helping your clients figure out what to do with their lives? Or are you transforming their lives by step-changing leadership skills and re-connecting them with their values, so that they can lead and communicate on a higher level?

HOW DO YOU KNOW WHAT VALUE THAT REPRESENTS TO YOUR CLIENT?

Simple. Ask. When you are talking about their end goals, goals that are aligned to and supported by values, ask what that is worth to them. How would it feel when they imagine that they've achieved their goals? If it doesn't feel like a million bucks, then you need to tell a better story! If you have a corporate client, make sure that you understand how this project is tied with your client's annual goals and how the organization will value this work.

PACKAGE YOUR SERVICE IN EXCEPTIONAL VALUE

If you are providing services to an executive or to an organization, show your recommended package as one of three options. For each of the two non-preferred options, take out features and benefits, so that these lower-priced options give less value (You wouldn't want the lower priced option to give the same or more value, right?).

Make the cost of NOT working with you clear. What are the risks in dollar terms? If you are a risk management consultant, then the risk of catastrophic business failure is obvious. But even for a sales training organization, the opportunity cost of lost sales has a dollar amount.

When you are talking, you need to become a storyteller, capable of eliciting pictures for your client, making them vivid and emotionally-connected to your audience. Once people know what end benefit they want, and they can imagine that clearly in their minds, and they know what it's worth, only then can you talk about prices. Don't fall into the trap of talking about prices too early. And never apologize for them.

Having said all of this, it is important to make sure that you look at your cost price and charge more than it costs you. You definitely don't want to be losing money bringing your good works into the world!

Laura Babeliowsky was trapped by her beliefs that people wouldn't be willing to pay a higher amount for her services. It took a transformation to change her fees from 300 euro to 8,000 euro.

I had 7,000 people on my list, and I made only 200,000 euro. I decided to join a coaching program. It's not easy to be in a coaching program; it's very confronting. My coach said, "Laura, your prices are much too low. You have to raise them." I said, "Okay, I have to do that." That was so scary; you cannot believe how scared I was. For three months, I was totally scared and also depressed because of the change. I started to raise my prices and clients said, "Oh, no, it's too much."

I was really out of my comfort zone, but I just did it. I remember doing an event in 2011. I had 40 people, and I offered a program for 7,000 euro. Only one person was interested, maybe. Nobody else. It was terrible!

But I continued, and I remember a person called me a few months later and said, "Oh, I want to do your program." I told him, "It's 8,000 euro," and he said, "Okay, that's fine." I thought, wow, that's the way it works. You just do it, and at a certain point, the client says yes. That's the new reality; you create a new reality just by doing it!

WHY INVESTING IN YOURSELF HELPS YOU AND YOUR CLIENTS

Have you noticed that when you pay more for something, you take it more seriously?

When you move from paying for a thing to investing in yourself, your perception of the value of what you are paying for increases exponentially.

For a female business owner, investing in yourself often takes the form of education or mentoring. You are the asset. Where a more traditional business might invest in capital assets like machinery or plant equipment, today's female entrepreneurs are the key asset of the business, so they need to invest and up-level themselves.

Investing in yourself works not just for you but for your clients as well. When you charge more for your services, then two very powerful things happen. Firstly, you're asking yourself to level up in terms of what you offer your clients. Secondly, you are asking your clients to take themselves more seriously. Let's go back a step and think about this in more detail.

WHEN YOU LEVEL UP

You start offering your packages based on results. You stop talking about the process of what you do, and you start talking about what happens at the end when your clients work with you.

You start investing in yourself and in your systems. You look at what you are doing in your business, and you start to think about what your clients would expect.

WHEN YOU ASK YOUR CLIENTS TO TAKE THEMSELVES MORE SERIOUSLY

This is where the magic really happens. When your clients make an investment, they expect to see a return that is greater than their dollar amount. They are more willing to do the work. They are more willing to devote time to thinking and reflecting and excavating their own stuff. They follow through. They follow you up! They really care because they have more skin in the game. They see you as an investment and not just as a cost.

YOUR EXERCISE

Have a look at what you're charging now. If it's not completely exciting, then consider what would happen if you were to significantly increase your rates. I don't just mean 5–10 percent. I mean significantly increase your rates, like triple them. What would you have to offer? What type of clients would you attract?

What would you have to do to help your clients feel that they are investing in themselves, rather than paying for a service? If that makes you completely excited, then take some time out and start planning what would have to be included in your package. Start playing around with the price. Set yourself a date to have it ready by.

RECEIVING

Do you like receiving money? If the answer to that is no, then how do you feel about receiving compliments? Do you try to reflect them back to the person who is trying to give you something? Receiving is an incredibly useful talent to develop.

When I ask clients how they arrive at their pricing, they often answer that they don't know, and it's because they don't value themselves enough to charge more. Or they simply say it's a lack of self-worth. Nobody (other than women who have built seven figure businesses) has said to me, "Well, I dramatically increased my prices, and people still see it as an excellent value given the transformation I can do."

What is self-worth? It's part of the self-esteem family. If you hold yourself in high esteem, you'll find it easy to say, "I am worthy" (self-respect), or, "I am competent" (personal capacity).

So often, the clients that I work with are happy to describe themselves as competent and ambitious but are reluctant to describe themselves as worthy. If my magic wand could fix just one problem, I would give all people a strong sense of self-worth and confidence in who they are. We are all born with a sense of self-worth, but over time, we let ourselves be chipped away. It starts before we even know what is happening, and it becomes a normal thing for us.

Women spend time engaging in activities that don't support a sense of high self-worth, such as perfectionism, heavy self-criticism, excessive willingness to please, and comparing themselves to others. Perfectionism can be an issue as it leads to frustration when perfection is not achieved (which it often can't be!). Heavy self-criticism means that it becomes hard to move forward and to take risks that might propel a new level of success. The excessive willingness to please means that we don't always have the right conversations with clients or team members, which means that we end up in a situation where we try not hurt the other person's feelings, and we don't protect our own boundaries. We have a fear of not being liked, but our clients and team members would actually benefit from having a leader around who is very clear about what should or needs to be happening instead.

The final damaging behavior of a low sense of self-worth is comparing yourself to others. That insidious little voice that says, "She's gone further along in her business than me, and we started at the same time. That means I'm not as good." "She's got a bigger client; she's better than me." None of these things are true, and they're certainly not true of what the future can hold. But saying them can constrain your growth and the growth of the business.

Your self-worth is a made-up story. There is no judge out there who has the authority to confer that sort of sentence on you. There is no point in time that you get lined up and touched by a wand labelled "worthy" or "unworthy." It just doesn't happen, which means it comes to you from you.

You can decide to be worthy. Today.

Even if you don't believe it just yet, do yourself a favor and act as though you were worthy. If you pretend (or know) that you are worthy, what would you do differently with your business? Your clients? How would you value your time? And how would you value your invoicing and getting paid a fabulous amount on time?

INVESTING IN YOUR BUSINESS

Investing is how you leverage money to achieve a better financial outcome. Women who continue to grow as entrepreneurs invest in their businesses and they invest in themselves.

Investing in the business means implementing systems that allow you to expand your personal capacity. The next chapter will go into more detail. It might include hiring a team who is able to amplify the message of your business. It might be purchasing and implementing a technical system that can automate your marketing or invoicing. It might even be a telephone system that integrates with your CRM and allows for voice broadcasts.

In the same way that the business can be made to run more smoothly, your personal growth must be nurtured and invested in. It's possible to undergo transformation by yourself, but it is a longer path, and it's fraught with heartache and doubt.

Your investment in yourself can be made in time or money. It's critical that if you do decide to invest that you take action. You need to be invested enough, and you need to be committed enough that you take yourself and your own growth seriously. You need to be called upon to step up and become the person that you want to be.

Carey Peters has made a commitment to herself over the next year of her growth.

Over the next year, I want to take the stopper off my own growth. In my experience, it's easier said than done. Because if it was, I'd be doing it already if it was safe to do so. But for some reason, it hasn't been. So, for me, it's about uncovering those reasons and then transforming them, so that I can allow myself more.

CHAPTER SUMMARY

* Money is energy and a valuable tool for living the life you want.

* Money will help you expand your business contribution, taking your lifestyle up a level, or increasing your philanthropy.

* Your income is only limited by what you believe you can earn.

* Develop your skill at selling as soon as you can and continue to build on it. It makes your business attractive to money.

* Review your pricing regularly to ensure it reflects your value.

* Invest in yourself and grow your skill set and your mindset to be where you want your business to be in the future.

BONUS DOWNLOADS

Visit the exclusive resources section of the book at
www.oneextrazero.com/catapult/bonus

Take the downloadable assessment and discover how strong is your Catapult: A Woman's 7-Figure Business Quotient.

Download a Guided Exercise to Explore Your Money Beliefs.

CHAPTER 7

LEVERAGE YOURSELF WITH TIME AND TEAM

Time is your most precious gift because you only have a set amount of it. You can make more money, but you can't make more time. When you give someone your time, you are giving them a portion of your life that you'll never get back. Your time is your life. That is why the greatest gift you can give someone is your time.

> —Rick Warren, The Purpose Driven Life: What on Earth Am I Here for?

Your ability to grow your business is driven by your ability to turn time into money. You might also leverage your time through employing other people, or creating a product that can be leveraged through turnover or royalties, but it all starts with your time.

As your business grows, there's only so much you can take before the demands on your time overwhelm you, and your mind and body break! There is only so much time in the day, and you need to spend your time building your business rather than pure operations. To do that, you'll need to look at what team you need to have in place. You'll also need a plan for how to bring them into your unique culture and have them thrive.

You are the leader of the business. You can never abdicate responsibility for the vision of the business, for the clients' satisfaction, and for the culture of the place. These are yours, and as the leader, you need to shape the environment so that the business can benefit from having these people who want to help you share and amplify your message.

TIME – THE KEY TO YOUR SUCCESS

Successful people, and especially women with multi-million dollar businesses, know that time is their most valuable asset. How they spend their time, and how they focus their attention during their working hours, determines their results.

I was reluctant when it came to my own interest in time management. When I was fresh from the university, I wanted to be a free spirit, carried where impulse and desire took me, relying on intuition to tell me where and what I should be attending to.

My first major shift came when I realized that my intuition didn't often take my goals into account; I was quite whimsical and prone to beer and skittles, but then I started to take a different view of my time.

The most recent shift was when I realized that Oprah, Leonardo da Vinci, and Steve Jobs had the same amount of time as I did. Twenty-four hours in the day. Nothing more and nothing less. They might have more people helping them now, and they might have more resources available to them, but when they started out, they had no more leverage than I did.

The other thing that should be acknowledged is that we rarely have more than 40,000 days available to us, and many of us have closer to 30,000 days. When you consider where you are in your life and just how many of these days you have left, you might start to consider the importance of those remaining days. They really are all you have!

Your relationship with time is crucial. You need to give it love and attention now because it will continue on regardless. You can't get back today or this week, let alone this moment. It is a truism that wherever you focus your attention, your energy will follow. If you aren't achieving your goals, go back and look at your calendar and see how much time you are dedicating towards activities that support your goals. There's a very good chance that your time is being directed away from where it needs to be.

Carey Peters carefully defends her time, knowing that she only has so much of it.

I'm extremely rigorous about how I schedule myself. Even as I say that I hear in my head, 'Well, you could still be more rigorous,' and that's true. I don't even keep a to-do list anymore; anything that has to be done by me goes right on my calendar, so that there's nothing that's sitting around waiting for me. I just get things taken care of.

THE VALUE OF YOUR TIME

Dan Kennedy includes an exercise in the first chapter of his book, No B.S. Time Management for Entrepreneurs, which changes the way that people think about their time. I'll share a version of it here.

Take your base earnings target for the year; let's say it's $500,000. A lot of business owners don't know what their earnings targets are for the year, but given that the purpose of a business is to generate revenue and profit, let's make up a number. Note that the base earnings target is not the same as the base income target. The earnings are the revenue that the business turns over; the income is the amount of money left over after you have paid all of the costs. Depending on the business, this income number is generally dramatically different than the earnings number.

Base earnings target = _____

x 1.8 (tax and miscellaneous costs) =_____

Divided by 220 days of work = _____

Divided by eight hours per day = _____

Amount you are worth per hour = _____

But, let's say that only one-third of your time is spent productively. For those hours, your time is worth:

Amount you are worth per hour times three: _____

WHAT ARE YOUR HIGHEST VALUE ACTIVITIES?

"Your ability to channel energy into your highest value activities will determine your rewards in life."
—David Keane

Your highest value activities are those that value your time the most. One of the challenges for business owners who've started from scratch is that they CAN do almost everything in the business, because, in the beginning, they had to. They know how to pack the boxes, find new ink for the printer, and even tally up their balance sheets.

At some stage though, your time is going to be valued at a higher rate than those tasks can provide. If your charge-out rate is closer to $300 per hour or $3,000 per hour, then it doesn't make financial sense to be working on tasks that someone charging $30 per hour can do.

Quite often your highest value activities are generating new business through face-to-face meetings with clients or working one-on-one with high-end clients. If you are able to generate significant revenue through these meetings and project work, then you will need to maximize the number of these and minimize the amount of time you spend organizing the meeting time and location, or even finding the new leads to have meetings with.

You won't want to abdicate your marketing and content generation entirely. These are the messages by which your audience will know you, and they create the impression of your brand in their eyes. But you'll want to train yourself not to start from scratch each time. Having an assistant help you, or an expert external writer, can accelerate the time from your initial thoughts to having the final material ready to go. You will still need to be involved in giving direction, judging the quality, providing feedback, and authorizing the final approval. However, you will free yourself from a great deal of writing and editing.

PRODUCTIVITY

Once you know what your goals are, and you have strategies in place to help you get there, you will end up with projects big and small. You still have all of the ongoing administration work and the client delivery work (or sourcing the product). You now need to figure out what to do first.

Generally, it's the income-producing activities. These are the things that determine your ability to stay in business. You will be bombarded with a lot of things that you can do, but only some of these things will bring you in money today, and only some of the things will bring you in money tomorrow. As the CEO of your business, your role is to delegate or destroy all tasks that do not bring in value.

FOCUS IS CRITICAL TO YOUR SUCCESS

"The abundance of books is a distraction."
    – Seneca the elder

The challenge of focusing and staying focused is not a new problem. However, effective solutions exist, and you can learn to excel.

Knowing your goals and committing to getting them is one thing. You also want to be focused enough to follow through. It's easy to be distracted in business. You can be distracted from your task on a micro-level. Telephones, social media, and thoughts of your to-do list might interrupt any intense conversation or period of intense work. It takes just a moment to be interrupted, but it can take up to 30 minutes to get back into the swing and momentum of the work.

Andrea Culligan can see a future where focus becomes an increasingly important part of the picture. She wants to build a more unified business with less fragmentation than in the past.

The end game is that the focus is about working strongly in the strategic and branding space with very good companies, and we've already started to transition those over for the next 12 months. But that's not just about employment branding, we also do front of house branding, retail branding, and we're starting to see those two things converge, which is beautiful. We meet and talk to a company about the brand that they are posing outside to the customer, and how that has a huge impact on the inside of the business. We're focusing on becoming the thought leaders within that space and creating much more authentic brands for many other companies. Offering focused and stabilized growth.

You might even be focused on the wrong activities. Looking at the wrong measures on a regular basis can send you well off-track from your goal. If you are trying to create in one area that you think is your strategic focus, you might miss the opportunity to reframe the problem.

INFORMATION OVERLOAD

Information overload refers to the amount of available information being greater than the brain's ability to comprehend and process the information. The deluge of information on Twitter, daily updated websites, books, and in the 24 hour news cycle means that it's not possible to keep up with the core facts being presented or the commentary on it. It's so easy to be caught up by the information that other people are producing that you forget on what your own goals are.

You might have also come across this while researching on the Internet. You have given yourself half an hour to look for good holiday destinations, and you look at a couple of places that seem right up your alley. You then notice a little link to the blog, where you can see a recent wedding, and you wonder if it's really that idyllic. You look at the pictures – ahhh – you sigh and see a link to vote for this wedding in Easy Weddings of the Year. You follow that through and see photos of one wedding on horseback. "That can't be easy," you think to yourself. Then, you notice up in the top right hand corner a customized ad to your browser's history. "I forgot about that book!" And then there you are, filling up your cart with auto-suggestions.

MICRO-INTERRUPTIONS

This is where you are working on a task and the phone rings, so you answer it. It takes someone somewhere between 20–30 minutes to get back into their work, even if it was a just a brief interruption. If the task is not time-bound, it can take up to 50 percent longer to complete. If you're under a deadline, you might find the task still gets completed in the same amount of time, but research has shown that the quality of the work decreases markedly as less deep thinking takes place and more mistakes are made.

In roughly one out of five cases, the interruption completely prevents you from getting back to the task that same day. You might find that the interruption reminds you to get up and go to the bathroom or to check your social media or make some lunch. The best ways of avoiding interruptions is to set up clear boundaries such as an energetic do-not-disturb sign. You can turn off email notifications, disconnect yourself from the Internet and work offline, turn your phone off or unplug it from the wall. Hiding is also very effective. If people can't find you because you're working in the public library, then you're less likely to be interrupted. If you know you need to get something done, the best way is to not be interrupted.

Internet marketing Dan Kennedy is brutal about refusing to give in to interruptions. His hard-line approach is inspiring, and if you make it only 30 percent of the way along the path to where he is, you will have an astonishing step-change in your approach to time. Operating a multi-million dollar enterprise, he relies on the fax (no email) to communicate and finds that people disturb him less often and with better-planned communications.

MACRO-INTERRUPTIONS

Bright Shiny Object syndrome is where you chase all that is new and shiny. The dangerous impact is that you don't finish what you start, and, because you don't finish, you don't achieve your goals. The first step is to recognize and take responsibility for your own patterns.

Let's say that you've identified your primary goal for the year, and you've also identified the key bodies of strategic work that will get you there. You start work on a project that delivers against your strategies and after about three months, you get most of the way in. Only another three or four weeks to go before you're finished.

Then, a colleague calls and asks if you'd like to do a joint venture project – a workshop that combines the best of both of your abilities. You hesitate because you know you're onto a winner, but she's persuasive and has a great network, and you've wanted to work with her in the past. You both talk through what it could look like, and you've started to sell yourself on the idea of it. You shelve what you're working on and start to collaborate. You pick a date some months in the future, draw together an agenda, allocate responsibilities, and start to work on the content and marketing plans. A few months later, she loses interest as she's picked up another great project with such potential.

You pick yourself off the floor, stunned at the lack of commitment that people make to themselves and others, and look at where you left off. It's now almost six months since you started that first project, and although you only had three weeks to go on each project, you now have two unfinished projects and a sense of being emotionally sideswiped.

START WITH A PLAN AND WORK BACKWARDS

When is the best time to plant a 20-year-old tree? 20 years ago.
When is the second best time to plant a 20-year-old tree? Now.
—Chinese proverb

Given you know why you're doing what you do, and you know what your goals are for the year, the next step is to look at each of those goals separately and in detail. Start with each of the goals and work out what is involved in achieving each one. Let's say that you have four projects over the next six months, and they need to run concurrently. Let's say one might take six weeks worth of project-based work (i.e. not working on the project full time). Another might take three weeks, one nine weeks, and one twelve weeks. Make sure you include a buffer for the inevitable distractions and disruptions of life, let's say around 50 percent.

You'll want to put the dates that you want these finished into your calendar, and then work backwards from there. Your aim is to make your workload manageable, so that you don't end up with all four projects at the same time if possible. You also know when you want to start because you know when you want to finish.

PROJECT SOFTWARE

Generally, to estimate the time properly, it's ideal to map out all of the tasks. Some people use a piece of paper, others use software specifically designed for project management, such as Microsoft Project or a cloud solution such as Basecamp. Look out for whether you need a remote team to be able to access the project, or if it's likely that the list of tasks will expand as you know more about the work that's being done. Give each of these tasks times.

Now, put the hours into your calendar or day planner. Make it clear that this block of time is for this project. Keep these appointments as important meetings that cannot be over-ridden. This will take some discipline and will be easier to do if you value yourself.

If you don't feel that you have the discipline, do some research on how to develop discipline. It's the ability to do something that you know is important, and you want the results, even if you don't feel like it at that particular moment. There are effective techniques. Developing self-esteem is another critical factor. You can either do things that reinforce your sense of self-worth, such as showing up and doing the work, or, you can pretend to have high self-esteem. Say to yourself, "What would a woman who values herself do in this situation?" By pretending, you'll soon find that you do the work, and you'll be proud of what you do, and then you'll develop it. Fake it until you make it!

MULTITASKING

Multitasking refers to doing multiple things at one time. Most of the time, multitasking doesn't work.

Some people can genuinely do this in certain circumstances. For example, highly trained Morse code operators can have 100 percent accuracy while receiving or transmitting Morse code and while carrying on a verbal conversation. This is because the Morse code is over-learned; there is so little cognitive requirement that it is almost reflective.

But under almost every other circumstance, multi-tasking can't be done. It means that you do both or all of the tasks less well. It is far better to work on one task, and finish it completely (or at least put it away completely), and then move to the next one.

TIMETABLES/PLANNERS/TIME CHUNKING

A good planning system cannot be overestimated. Whether you decide to have a paper planner that covers a week at a time, a day planner, or an online calendar, it's important to know what you're doing and when. Keeping track of what your goals are, by what date you want to achieve them, and also when you're going to devote your attention to them, is critical to keeping pace.

Choose your planner carefully. Some people design their own as they become increasingly aware of what the areas are that they want to focus on daily.

Once you have your planner, consider how you are going to block off time. Scheduling meetings as they arise and then filling in the time around it is pretty inefficient. Start by scheduling the most important goals and projects. Then, allow meetings and other opportunities to be scheduled around this.

The most ruthless timekeepers don't have to-do lists. Everything that is to be done gets scheduled, delegated, or deleted.

And you might even want to consider an old-fashioned tickler filing system. They're not convenient if you travel a lot, but if they suit your working style, people's lives have been changed by them. Let's say that you have approximately 90 files, all marked with the 30 odd days for each month. The reminders of things you need to do go inside each file. Follow up invoices. Contact the people for your speaking gig in two months. As you move through and rotate each file daily, it tickles your memory!

TEAM

If you're serious about having a business rather than just a self-employed job, then you are going to want to bring a team on. You might choose to have a model where you bring in freelancers as needed, working on a contract hourly basis. Or you might look at a more traditional model, where you have you at the top.

As you grow your business, you need to decide pretty early on if you want to do everything, or if there are elements that you want to delegate.

Kendall SummerHawk has become increasingly aware of the value of her time and of the importance of having the right team in place to deliver against her most important goals. With a strong sense of purpose, Kendall needs to get her message out very clearly.

For team... For almost 30 years, I've had a history of being able to engender tremendous loyalty in my team. Back then I didn't have the wisdom, insight, or experience to hire a specialist, so I hired people who were also all in. Within a few years of starting out, I had one part-time virtual assistant, and she worked incredibly hard. All of my team works hard. They work very deeply; they pull all kinds of crazy hours, and they do whatever it takes to get the job done. Back in the beginning, I did a lot of things myself. I even did 1Shopping Cart myself!

Every time I made these investments, I gave up some of my tasks. The first task I gave up was answering email. I remember when my assistant's first bill came – it was $800, and I freaked out. It wasn't like I didn't have the money, but it felt like a huge chunk of my revenue at that time. I just bit the bullet and 'cowgirl'd up,' as we sometimes say, and said, 'I have to look beyond that expense. I have to look at the amount of money that I am going to be generating.' In that respect, I was very, very disciplined in forcing my thoughts to focus on the big picture.

The reasons to delegate are strong. If your time is worth hundreds or thousands of dollars an hour, then you shouldn't be running to the store to pick up more milk or your dry cleaning when someone can do that for you at a fraction of the cost.

You need to be ready to protect your time and force yourself into your highest value activities – the activities that bring you the biggest bang for your time.

PRIVILEGE OF HIRING

It really is such a privilege to hire another person as it not allows you to leverage someone else's time, it also allows you to amplify your message. It helps you to focus on your highest value activities.

The first team member that is often brought on board is administrative or bookkeeping support. You might hire this person on a part-time basis to free up a few hours of your week.

You need to be very clear that that time is being paid for out of your wallet. You've hired that person to be a member of your team for a reason, and it's so that you are able to use your time, not on that task, but on a bigger picture. That team member then has to be held responsible and accountable for delivering that work.

A great exercise is to look at the opportunity cost of not hiring that team member. You might find that if you have a few hours free per week, then you'll be able to follow up a prospective client, reach out for a speaking engagement, write an article, or plan out the next month of business building activities. Each of these activities might ultimately bring you far more income than the hourly cost of that team member.

Shelene Taylor now runs several massage clinics and high-end medical spas. She used to do everything, including cleaning out the Jacuzzi. But she now meets with her team once a month, and they are now able to open new stores without her. Shelene describes how she made that transformational journey.

I was like the Red Queen. I was very 'off with their heads,' instead of coming at it with a perspective that was humane and caring. I'm in this caring, nurturing business, but I wasn't really nurturing. I discovered that I was doing things in way that was shaped by my own filter, and I was then attracting people who were mirroring the things that I needed to deal with. I blamed them, and the truth was that I needed to shift who I was. I needed to take a look at how I was presenting to them.

It wasn't that I needed to be nice; I needed to be powerful and graceful. At the time, I didn't know that those two things could go together. I thought being powerful meant 'off with their heads.' I thank my first business coach for helping me make that transformation.

ARE YOU AVOIDING HIRING A TEAM AND DELEGATING?

You might feel that it's hard to delegate. If you want to grow your business substantially, then you will want to do some excavation around that. It will certainly be easier to grow your business if you have helping hands.

IT'S NOT CHEAPER AND EASIER TO DO IT YOURSELF

One of the reasons that women find it hard to delegate is that it seems easier and cheaper to do it themselves. Consider how much time it is going to take to do a task, and then consider how long it will take to find someone and then train that person to do exactly the same thing. "It'll be quicker just to do it myself," says the little voice inside your head.

Remember, if your time is worth hundreds or thousands of dollars an hour, it is not cheaper or easier to do something worth $30 an hour.

IT'S NOT JUST THE MONEY; IT IS ALL ABOUT THE TIME

It's not the time that it takes to do that task once that you're saving. It's delegating the repetitive tasks that allow your time to be freed up over the long term. You're looking to gain back hours, if not weeks of time, over the space of a year. If you consider that you can save one hour a day or five hours a week scheduling appointments, rescheduling appointments, responding to standard email enquiries, and similar tasks, then over the course of a 50 week year, you will have saved 250 hours, which is equivalent to more than six working weeks at 40 hours per week. You could design a new program, invest your time in more training, or read a book a week on your field in that time. You could reach out to significantly bigger clients, go to Bali, or have every Friday afternoon off to get away for the weekend. The point is that it gives you choices.

YOU ARE WORTHY OF HAVING A TEAM

Sometimes we don't delegate because we think that someone else won't enjoy the work, or that it's too menial. That's a self-worth issue right there. If this is work that you have been able to do, then someone else is able to do it. And if it is something like your bookkeeping, and you're embarrassed for a professional to see the state of your shoebox of receipts or the size of your income, you need to get over that right now. If you don't like it, or aren't good at doing it, that is exactly the task that needs to be outsourced now. As a result of giving that unwanted task to someone else, you free up your mind to be creative in other ways. You know that you are no longer weighed down by that albatross around your neck.

IT MIGHT BE YOUR EGO

You might think that you're actually the best at doing this task. You might be the best at thinking of excellent social media posts, carefully creating beautiful images that drive engagement, getting the font just right, and building a loyal following of fans dedicated to your continued social media presence (even if they don't buy anything). You've got to take a look at where you spend your time. Do you need to be spending 90 percent of your time on activities that generate new business or servicing existing customers? Is your social media presence creating a powerhouse of leads eager to buy? If not, then you have a couple of choices. You can invest in learning how to make social media lucrative, or you can delegate the task of updating your social media pages to somebody proficient in it. Or, ideally, you can do both.

ARE YOU AVOIDING RESPONSIBILITY?

A final reason that women sometimes avoid delegating is that they don't want to be responsible for someone else's income. You've got the sense that if somebody chooses to come and work for you, they don't have the full picture of the risky situation that they are getting themselves into. You're now responsible for this team member's ability to buy groceries and pay a mortgage. The truth is that you're not responsible for their choices. If you know that you are about to wind up your company in two months time, then you're probably not acting from a place of integrity when you lure someone away from an existing role where they have been happy for the past five years. But for the vast majority of hiring situations, if you believe that you have a business of good repute that needs additional help to continue growing, then you can't make the choice for another person about whether they are going to work with you or not.

Sophie Bartho found hiring to be less of a risk and more of a responsibility but an absolutely essential part to being able to leverage her graphic design business.

It comes down to confidence. The first time you hire someone, you think 'Oh, what if I can't keep paying him or her?' The first person I hired was Matt, and I didn't see it as a risk, but I saw it as a huge responsibility. The overlying emotional feeling at the time was by offering this person a job I was making a commitment, and I had to be able to deliver on that.

You think of the enormous responsibility, and then you realize, "Well, I can do this," and then you hire someone else. Then you think, "We need a bigger office," and that's another big commitment. Then, you realize you need more equipment, and it just keeps progressing. My growth was organic – we did it gradually in stages. I didn't have a business model or a strategic plan.

WHEN THE TEAM MEMBER ADDS SIGNIFICANT VALUE

Not all of your team is going to be administrative. Your first team member or even your fifth team member might be someone who interfaces with the client and delivers strategy work of an incredibly high caliber.

You need to be sure that the team member is able to amplify your message. If he or she has a different set of values, or believes that they have a message (different from yours), then you don't have to employ that person to do the work for you!

If you find the right people who amplify your message, they get your purpose, they think that what you are doing in the world is great, and they want to get on board and help you do that, then you are in a sweet spot. This is the ultimate privilege. You're able to direct the energy of someone who feels compelled to help you.

Natalie Archer hires exceptional team members who are high on achievement-orientation and value being on a team and collaborating. She recognizes that this is a strategic challenge to be solved.

Bringing on the team is the most important thing that I do. It is about hiring the people with the right fit in the first place. First, I look for people who are highly achievement-oriented and my reasons for this are firstly it's the most highly correlated capability with success in professional services firms, and secondly because in an unstructured environment that is purposefully low on management, I need people who are driven, strong on self-responsibility and thrive on freedom and opportunity. I'm 10 years into this now, and it is still true.

People who have a sharp intellect and are values driven, and probably quite entrepreneurial, don't mind unstructured environments and ambiguity. The team player element comes in really strong with people who are not driven just to individually succeed, but to be collaborative and supportive of other people in the team.

To nurture and support this environment, we came up with the BCD – Bendelta Cultural Delights. You can choose the hours and number of days that you work, where you work from, and take unpaid leave. Flexibility is key because life's too short. I think you should do things that really light you up, and I want to have people come and stay for a long period of time. It's all about personal responsibility, and that, to this day, has worked really, really well.

WHAT'S THE RIGHT STRUCTURE?

Employment laws are so individual by country or even state that it's not possible to say whether it is better to employ your team directly or to employ them as contractors. Your particular situation might even encourage a service agreement with a provider who hires the team members directly and then contracts the total business services to your business, so that they then handle payroll and legislative requirements for each individual team member who works on your business.

Know what it is that you are trying to build and start with small but determined steps.

KNOW THE SIZE OF YOUR TEAM

When you start your business, and again when you review the direction of your business, you're going to have a vision of where you want to take it. You're going to be able to imagine how many people you want to impact. You're going to be able to imagine whether this is through an offline or online model. Will you be working with tangible products or intangible services? Are they easily scaled? Will you be focusing more on sales, marketing, or production?

Not everyone wants to create the corporate behemoths that still wander the earth with tens of thousands of employees. There are a couple of businesses here which have hundreds on their payroll, and you can see many examples of profitable firms in this book who have somewhere between 10 and 40 people working for them. And I've met many more who have fewer than five people.

Know what your ideal size is, and then shape and direct your business to deliver that.

HOW TO CHOOSE A TEAM

Hiring a team can be a minefield for some, and having a couple of bad experiences early on can shatter your whole perception of how beneficial it is to have a team around.

The first principle is to understand in detail what the role is for. What tasks exactly do you want to outsource? Being clear that a good team member will be able to add value beyond your own knowledge is good, but you also need to give more guidance than, "I think I need some administrative help."

If you know that, you want to start with hiring a team member who is able to deliver some actual content work for you. Let's say, you are a consultant who wants to find another consultant to help with some of the more standard and low-risk work. You'll want to map out what work actually counts as standard or low-risk, how many hours you are likely to need help for, whether they are ever client-facing, what types of timelines they'll need to work to, and how often they will need to be available for project or team meetings with you. You'll also want to be clear on how available you will be to supervise them, and you'll also want to be aware of what their level of internal motivation and need for training needs to be.

This type of outline is essential, because as soon as you tell anyone what type of team member you want to hire, you'll find a wide variety of people who you know or you know through one or two degrees of separation who might be interested. If you don't know the criteria for hiring, then you're likely to hire someone who is available, rather than someone who meets the needs of the business.

Linda Simonsen recognized early on that her team needed to have the same values as she did, so that she could continue her brand promise of exceptional customer service.

There's no question that my business was built off my back because of my initial commitment to delivering amazing service. It didn't matter what time of day a customer called or what they asked for, I'd bend over backwards to make it happen. My goal over time has been to instil that same sort of culture in the business. So even if it is not me servicing the customer, they experience the same service.

That's been challenging at times because what a business owner or entrepreneur expects from a standards point of view is often much higher than what an employee is willing to give. So the one thing I've learned is as your business grows, it's really important to connect your people to your purpose and your vision. They need to feel that same passion for making a difference and what we stand for as I do; otherwise, the customer gets disappointed with the level of service that they receive.

HOW TO BRING TEAM INTO YOUR CULTURE

Every work environment has its own unique culture. You might think that you work just like everybody else, but you don't. You have expectations of yourself and of the team already around you that are like unwritten laws. This is the way that it should be done here.

Andrea Culligan has also learned from her early experience about bringing team on and integrating them into a particular culture and aligning them with a vision and manifesto.

I've always been incredibly passionate about making sure that our clients feel like a part of the family. I had an incredible focus on integrity, honesty, and transparency. Those were the values that I was working with, but I didn't have it all laid out in the beginning.

Now, we have a clear manifesto that everyone has to sign when they join the business. We all worked together to create it, we recruit according to it, and it explains how we work, who we are as people, what we believe in, and what's ok and what's not. We talk about it every month, what it has done for us, and what we have done that has exemplified the client service pillars that we believe in. That's how we recruit.

We're all artists in here; this is now a branding business. We've got designers and strategists, big thinkers and visionaries, but this is still a commercial environment.

I also believe that if you go through all the right processes, and your gut still tells you that it's not right, you should listen. Experience has taught me to listen more to myself and my energy and to be confident in that.

First of all, you need to bring new team members up to speed really quickly on what the culture of the place is. You absolutely can't assume that they will know just by looking around, and this is especially true if your team member is operating out of a virtual or remote location.

A good way to bring new team members on board is to have a formal induction process. You can share the mission of the business, how you came to start the business, the values of the business, and try to articulate the way that you operate. For example, if your team member has to go to the bank during her working hours, does she need to say that she's unavailable for that 25 minutes, or can she just go without giving notice?

You also want to articulate your style of leadership. Do you like to be close to the work, or are you happy to only review when close to completion? Are you task-oriented or results-oriented? What is your preference for interruptions – do you prefer to be interrupted for quick questions that let your team member keep working, or do you prefer that he or she moves on to something else, knowing that you'll be free within 90 minutes or so? There are very few wrongs or rights in this, but you should be able to share your individual style and how you expect others to accommodate your idiosyncrasies!

ONGOING BOUNDARIES

We've already mentioned boundaries in passing, such as how to view the salary or compensation, or whether someone needs to give you notice to go to the bank during lunch.

But you also have to look at what performance levels you will tolerate. If your team is there to help you grow your business and better serve your customers (as well as increase profit), then you want them to be delivering on that, as well as having a clear idea of what work actually needs to be done (remember, all work can expand to fill any space!). You're also going to want to have a clear idea of what business metrics this activity is going to impact.

You want data.

Is the investment that you are making in your team member giving you a good return? If you've hired salespeople, are they generating sales? Is it the amount that you were expecting to get? And what is the reason behind the numbers? You're looking for explanations, not excuses. If you're hearing that the numbers aren't where you want them to be, and your team members are telling you that it's not their fault, and, in fact, it is someone else's fault, then you need to decide up front how many excuses you want to hear. Obviously, if they had pneumonia and were in hospital on a drip for a week, you will need to adjust your expectations of their ability to make face-to-face calls that week. But if you're finding that there is an endless stream of little crises, then you have to ask how committed they are to growing your business.

GET COMFORTABLE HAVING TOUGH CONVERSATIONS

This is linked to leadership. Generally, you're not close friends with the people on your payroll. You're spending this much time together because you have a commercial arrangement. You respect each other, and you expect to have a strong working relationship. If things aren't working out the way you expected, then you'll want to take the lead and correct it quickly.

As a boss, your need to be liked needs to be less than your need for your business to do well. This doesn't mean to act like the Red Queen. Instead, consider that if you only had one day to fix this, what powerful and graceful conversation would you have?

Before you start this sort of conversation, you'll want to be clear on your desired outcome. Are you looking for improved performance, or are you looking to terminate the arrangement?

As you move through the conversation, you're looking for positive signs that your team members have received the feedback as a way to improve their results in a positive way. If your team members are defensive and consistently blaming others, while there might be a conspiracy against them, it is more likely that they have put themselves into victim mode.

Ariel Hyatt also went through a period of transformation with her team and now has learned that if she wants unconditional support from them, then she's going to get it.

I'm very careful with the relationships that I make now. I have finally learned how to get support. This is the lesson that I've heard a lot of people talk about, and it's so true – until you have real support, you will be stuck.

I always had one or two people that were on my staff that weren't doing a great job, and, instead of firing them, I would try to fix them. I think a lot of women can relate to this. It's a female tendency to believe that if something isn't working that it must have something to do with them.

I often found myself saying, 'Let's make the system better for you.' I now ask myself, 'What are you tolerating?' Toleration is not in any recipe for success. I finally got an assistant who is completely competent and capable, and she helps me schedule our interviews. She helps me with my calendar, the dishwasher, whatever I need help with. I actually have an entirely excellent staff now –not a weak link in the chain – it's literally the first time in my life I can say that. Everyone who works for me shows up and does a phenomenal job.

If you want to have outstanding support in your team, and in your business, then make sure you reach out and get it.

CHAPTER SUMMARY

* Your time is your most important asset.

* If you have a big vision, it's unlikely that you'll be able to do everything yourself using only your own time. Leverage other people's time.

* Choose your team from those who are delighted to amplify your message.

* Be aware of any resistance about your ability to delegate to team and ask what a CEO would do.

BONUS DOWNLOADS

Visit the exclusive resources section of the book at
www.oneextrazero.com/catapult/bonus

Take the downloadable assessment and discover how strong is your Catapult: A Woman's 7-Figure Business Quotient.

Download the Opportunity Cost Template for Hiring Team.

CONCLUSION

As I came to this part of the book, I spent some time trying to crystallise the message that I wanted to give to you. The single idea that you must take away if this book is to help you on build a 7-figure business. The idea is:

The inner work <u>must</u> come before the outer work.

That is why every chapter has been laid out in such a way that the mindset, or the approach, to business is discussed first, and then the Down To Business section, with the practical business building aspects come second.

It feels incredible to come to the final chapter. It seems like such a rich body of work, a mix of mindset and practical business building advice. I've been so delighted to be here with you on this journey. There is so much that I want to share with you about creating your 7-figure business.

I really hope that reading this book has inspired you to start making some shifts in the way that you approach your business. I hope you are on your way to making your next transformational steps in your growth and that of your business.

I want to leave you with a few last thoughts on continuing your success. I just love the thought of women having the independence that they so deserve. And I want you to have that. The ability to have choices. The person that you have to become, who is such a higher version of yourself. The person you always wanted to be, but somehow didn't think it was possible.

CELEBRATE YOUR SUCCESSES

It's easy to get caught up in the challenges and the busyness of the day. Do stop, though, and recognise the distance that you have come already. Women are notorious for trying to under-play their own achievements. It's like we want to somehow become smaller and less noticeable. For the vast majority of business types, it is not desirable to be less noticeable.

When you look back at over the past year or so, think about what you wanted to get done, and what you actually did get done. Take note of the new work that you brought on board. The clients who gave you feedback about the great work that you did. The steps you took to raise your profile, the level of investment your clients make in you and the quality of your work.

Don't lose sight of where you want to go. Recognise though that every step you take along the path brings you closer. You need to celebrate that you are steadily moving, maybe not always in the straightest of lines, but you are steadily moving towards your goal.

BUILDING A 7-FIGURE BUSINESS IS POSSIBLE

The women interviewed in this book, and the women who have built 7-figure businesses around you are amazing role models. Some started early. Some started later. Whilst a couple had access to incredible resources, most came from very modest beginnings. The level of formal education seems irrelevant. Some are single, and some have incredibly supportive partners. Along the way, I met single mothers with dramatic businesses, happily married childless couples and everything in the way. Not every story is in here. But there is no unifying factor.

The most important factor is your desire to get to where you want to be, and your ability to get back up again when the inevitable challenges arise.

Think about what it would mean for you to have a 7-figure business. For you, is it about the flexibility and freedom associated with that? It might be a measure of success that you've always wanted to attain. Or perhaps you strongly resonate with the person that you'd have to become to get there.

THE INEVITABLE CHALLENGES REALLY ARE CHALLENGES

I don't want to understate the challenges that arise along the way. As your business builds, the challenges don't go away.

You need to be aware that the challenges that come up at the start of the journey are different than those that come later. However, they will still seem to have the same impact and weight of punch behind them.

Some of them are predictable, not in the specific nature of

the challenge, but in the type. For example, at some stage, you will have a client who is not happy with your work. The details of whether it is your fault or their fault will be mostly irrelevant. You can decide in advance how you deal with customer complaints. You might decide to develop a way that you want to deal with complaints and develop a refunds policy ahead of time.

If you know what your values are and you're able to communicate these and embed these into everything that you do in the business, you will ahead by leaps and bounds.

INTERNAL CHALLENGES CAN BE THE TOUGHEST

Other challenges will be less predictable. These are quite often the internal challenges. The beliefs that you start to knock up against as you move outside of your comfort zone.

These are the beliefs that are strong like the tiny rope that holds the elephant in place. We don't know how to break through the ropes that have held us in place for so long. We can't see them, and so we don't see that they are there, we just see that we haven't been able to move past them.

THE INNER WORK COMES BEFORE THE OUTER WORK

The beliefs that brought you to where you are today cannot take you to where you want to be. The beliefs that brought you to today come from the past. They were useful in the past. They might not be useful in the future.

The beliefs that you need to hold to get you into the next stage of your journey will be different. Your beliefs around your value, your time and your ability to impact the world will continue to shift. It is possible to accelerate these mindshifts.

Without doubt, you will need to grow and transform as a person.

BE SURE TO GRAB YOUR TOOLBOX!

There are some extraordinary resources as part of this book. These have been made available to you for download at your convenience.

The first download to grab is your "Catapult: a 7-Figure Business Assessment". This will review the different areas covered in this book, starting with your purpose and finishing with your time and team. The format is a little unusual, but it works out super-well.

If you've decided that you want to build a 7-figure business, then you need to take committed action, in the right places.

Visit the exclusive resources section of the book at www.oneextrazero.com/catapult/bonus

* Take the downloadable assessment and discover how strong is your Catapult: A Woman's 7-Figure Business Quotient.

* And Access Other Valuable Business Building Material

ACKNOWLEDGEMENTS

This book would not have been possible without the generosity of the women interviewed for the book. Thank you so much for trusting me to tell your stories.

In alphabetical order:

* *Natalie Archer (Bendelta)*
* *Laura Babeliowsky (Bouw Een Bloeiend Bedrijf)*
* *Sophie Bartho (ex-SBA Design)*
* *Leela Cosgrove (Strategic Anarchy)*
* *Andrea Culligan (Unimail)*
* *Ariel Hyatt (CyberPR)*
* *Carey Peters (Holistic MBA)*
* *Linda Simonsen (FuturePeople)*
* *Kendall SummerHawk (Kendall SummerHawk)*
* *Shelene Taylor (Rubs)*

Thank you to Ruth Klein who helped shaped the book. To Nikki Griffiths who pulled out all stops to make my writing readable, and to Vanessa Maynard who has created the most beautiful cover design and layout.

Thank you also to my patient family who watched me write this book over the Sydney summer with many fewer trips to the beach. You are so loved and appreciated!

Made in the USA
Lexington, KY
22 April 2014